CASE STUDIES IN
EDUCATION AND CULTURE

General Editors

GEORGE *and* LOUISE SPINDLER

Stanford University

GROWING UP
IN A PHILIPPINE BARRIO

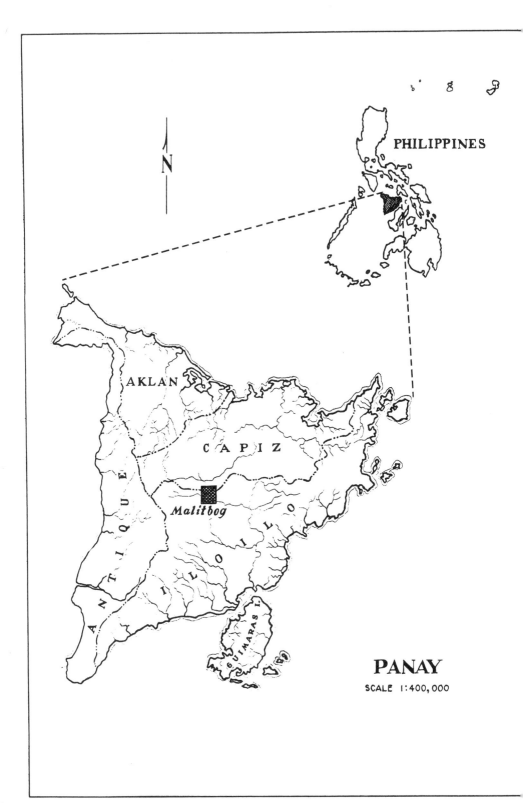

PHILIPPINES

PANAY

SCALE 1:400,000

AKLAN

CAPIZ

ANTIQUE

ILOILO

■ Malitbog

GUIMARAS I.

(N. Escultura—196?)

GROWING UP
IN
A PHILIPPINE BARRIO

F. LANDA JOCANO
University of the Philippines

HOLT, RINEHART AND WINSTON
New York • Chicago • San Francisco • Atlanta
Dallas • Montreal • Toronto • London • Sydney

Foreword

About the Series

This series of case studies in education and culture is designed to bring to students in professional education and in the social sciences the results of direct observation and participation in educational process in a variety of cultural settings. Individual studies will include some devoted to single classrooms, others will focus on single schools, some on large communities and their schools; still others will report on indigenous cultural transmission where there are no schools at all in the Western sense. Every attempt will be made to move beyond the formalistic treatments of educational process to the interaction between the people engaged in educative events, their thinking and feeling, and the content of the educational process in which they are engaged. Each study will be basically descriptive in character but since all of them are about education they are also problem oriented. Interpretive generalizations are produced inductively. Some are stated explicitly by the authors of the studies. Others are generated in the reader's mind as hypotheses about education and its environmental relationships.

The cross-cultural emphasis of the series is particularly significant. Education is a cultural process. Each new member of a society or a group must learn to act appropriately as a member and contribute to its maintenance and, occasionally, to its improvement. Education, in every cultural setting, is an instrument for survival. It is also an instrument for adaptation and change. To understand education we must study it as it is—imbedded in the culture of which it is an integral part and which it serves.

When education is studied this way, the generalizations about the relationship between schools and communities, educational and social systems, education and cultural setting that are current in modern educational discussions become meaningful. This series is, therefore, intended for use in courses in comparative and overseas education, social foundations and the sociology of education, international educational development, culture and personality, social psychology, cultural dynamics and cultural transmission, comparative sociology—wherever the interdependency of education and culture, and education and society, is particularly relevant.

We hope these studies will be useful as resources for comparative analyses, and for stimulating thinking and discussion about education that is not confined by one's own cultural experience. Without this exercise of a comparative, transcultural perspective it seems unlikely that we can acquire a clear view of our own educational experience or view education in other cultural settings without ethnocentric bias.

About the Author

F. Landa Jocano is an associate professor of anthropology at the University of the Philippines. He received his Ph.D. degree in 1963 from The University of Chicago. Before coming to the University of the Philippines, he was senior anthropologist at the National Museum and professorial lecturer at Centro Escolar University, both in Manila, Philippines. Since 1955 Professor Jocano has engaged in field research among various Philippine linguistic groups, including street-corner gangs in a slum district of urban Manila. His interests in field research range from social structure, socialization, small-group organization, community development, culture change, and prehistory. He has published numerous articles in professional journals, and among his books are: *The Sulod Society, Epic of Labaw Donggon,* and *The Traditional World of Malitbog: A Study of Community Development and Culture Change in a Philippine Barrio.*

About the Book

Growing Up in a Philippine Barrio is one of a few of its kind in the literature of anthropology and its emerging subfield, the anthropology of education. Written by a native of the Philippines, it is an analysis of education in its broadest sense—as socialization and enculturation rather than formal instruction in schools. It is also a detailed ethnography of life in a barrio on the island of Panay, one of the Bisayas, of the central Philippines.

The author has adopted as the framework for his analysis the life cycle of the individual from birth to death. This framework takes his analysis into nearly every aspect of community and personal life. He keeps close to the people of Malitbog by providing anecdotes and direct observation of individuals behaving in a variety of relevant contexts.

In the perspective of the total educational experience of the child, the four years of formal schooling provided in the government-supported school seem almost trivial. There is continuity provided by the community, but discontinuity between the school and the community. Given this discontinuity, it is inevitable that children will forget what they have learned in school as they grow up. It is apparent from Dr. Jocano's analysis that the peer group is of particularly great importance as a milieu for socialization; that it is community centered, not school centered; that it acts as a major mechanism of social control; and that it far outweighs the influence of any formal educational process in Malitbog.

The author also provides an analysis of kinship and of social relations in Malitbog, moving from family and household to the wider circle of kin and, finally, to the sanctions underlying the social order in the form of value orientations. Particularly notable as an example of the way in which the concepts and methods of anthropology can contribute to an understanding of education is the author's demonstration of how the social organization is in itself an educational institution and process.

The case study ends with analyses of the supernatural world and the treatment of death and burial, showing how they are aspects of culture learned by children who are present at all important events and who are taught to fear supernatural beings as a means of social control.

The study in its entirety is a demonstration, in adequate detail, of the ways in which infants become members of adult society and bearers of the culture of that society. We of the Western world, and particularly in America, need to look carefully into such processes. The crisis of alienation that grips us is raising serious questions about the functioning of our own methods of socialization and of education. The answers, for us, are not to be found in this study of a small, rural, Philippine barrio, but they may be found within the larger area of understanding to which this case study is a contribution. The purpose of these studies is to help develop a comprehensive, comparative overview of the human condition as relevant to the ways in which humans are educated.

George and Louise Spindler
General Editors
SAN DIEGO
ESTEPONA, SPAIN, 1969

Preface

.

The data for this study are based on fieldwork carried out intermittently among the farmers of Malitbog from 1955 to 1965. My initial visits to the barrio from 1955 to 1958 were financed by the Central Philippine University and the Asia Foundation as part of my project on folklore in central Panay. The second trip was in 1959–1960 and was supported by a grant-in-aid from the National Research Council of the Philippines and the National Museum as part of the project on Panay ethnography. The most intensive of these series of field studies was the one carried out in 1964–1965, under the sponsorship of the Community Development Research Council of the University of the Philippines. I wish to acknowledge my indebtedness to these institutions, without whose assistance this volume would never have been written. In preparing this report I am indebted to different persons. I wish to thank the Community Development Research Council for permission to quote from my monograph *The Traditional World of Malitbog: A Study in Community Development and Culture Change in a Philippine Barrio*. Special credit is due to the members of the Council for their valuable criticisms of my early reports. Their comments made me aware of a number of aspects of Malitbog social life which I would not have inquired into had they not brought these to my attention. To my colleagues at the National Museum and at the University of the Philippines I owe an abiding gratitude for stimulating exchanges of ideas about the subject matter presented in this book. I wish to acknowledge, in this connection, my gratitude to former National Museum Director Galo B. Ocampo for giving me so much assistance and time, while I was still with the National Museum, to write up my materials. Credit goes to Mauro Garcia for reading the earlier drafts of this book; many of his suggestions are incorporated here.

For the formal training which prepared me to undertake this study, I wish to thank Fred Eggan and E. D. Hester of the Philippine Studies Program, The University of Chicago, and Robert B. Fox, chief anthropologist of the Philippine National Museum. Last, I am most grateful to my wife, Adria P. Jocano, for her assistance in the field and in writing this book; she has always been my constant critic and source of encouragement.

F. Landa Jocano

Quezon City, Philippines
February 1969

Contents

GROWING UP
IN A PHILIPPINE BARRIO

Introduction

THIS BOOK is a case study in education. Because education, culture, and society are so intimately linked, it is also an ethnography. The various phases in the life cycle of farmers in Malitbog, a small barrio located in the central region of Panay island, Philippines (see accompanying map), are described, and the techniques of cultural learning and transmission in the community are analyzed. Central to this descriptive analysis of barrio life is the assumption that all relevant aspects of a culture are acquired by a child from his elders and peers, as he grows up, and in turn are transmitted by him, with modifications, to his own children. Educators have always been concerned about this process, although they have focused much of their attention on the acquisition of knowledge and skills through formal instruction in schools. However, schools are not universal, and in many nonliterate societies they are not necessary in the traditional forms of those societies. In societies where schools are important, as in Malitbog, these institutions constitute only a part of the educational system. A great deal of learning takes place outside of classrooms; knowledge and skills are acquired informally, through daily habituation at home, interaction with playmates in the neighborhood, and through watching adults at work.

Considered in this broad sense, education is more than formal schooling. It embraces all learning that necessitates the acquisition of culturally defined and effective ways of accommodating oneself to living as a member of a society. It begins early in childhood and continues throughout adult life. The process of imparting knowledge and skills is partly deliberate and partly unplanned in that instruction is often carried on intentionally through such activities as the chores at home and in the field, and occurs unintentionally in peer groups, by observation of adult behavior that is not meant as a model, and so forth. Social scientists label this process enculturation, socialization, or child rearing. Whichever term is used to describe it, education from this standpoint means learning of techniques for adjusting to the social environment from sources other than schools, colleges, and universities, as well as within the framework provided by these institutions (where they exist). These sources include interaction with members of the family, kin, friends, and acquaintances; with institutions like the church, government bureaucracy, clubs, and business concerns; and with the mass media like the newspapers, magazines, journals, books, televisions radios, and motion pictures. All of these sources wield influence in forming opinions, attitudes, values, and behavior among the people.

1

In a peasant community like Malitbog where modern mass media are lacking, myths, tales, songs, proverbs, and gossip constitute means through which learning is facilitated and social control exemplified. This body of traditional knowledge is reinforced by strong emphasis on strict observance of social usages, such as reciprocal obligations between kin, respect for elders, food exchanges between neighbors, behavior during public occasions, and the like. All of these culturally defined usages and ideas make up an informal curriculum for the education of children, a reservoir of knowledge from which the people draw much guidance for their day-to-day activities.

Seen from this standpoint, there is much that anthropologists and educators can learn from each other. To begin with, anthropology and education, as disciplines, are interested in learned behavior; both also consider early training as vitally important for the integration of the individual to society. Aside from this limited problem, however, anthropologists also study the social organization of the community as a whole. Educators may thus find anthropological studies useful in dealing with general education problems such as are posed by the following questions: How can the school be made functionally relevant to the community? What methods of instruction can be utilized in classrooms that will transfer productively and effectively the newly acquired knowledge and skills to conditions outside of the school? How and to what extent can the curricula of schools be made compatible with the values of the community?

One way to clarify the problem of the "classroom-community" continuum is first to know more about the learning process taking place outside of schools and to examine its relationship with what is being taught in classrooms. Children spend more time at home than in school, and parents, as part of their adult responsibilities, bring up their children in more or less the same way as they themselves were brought up. A knowledge of this process is useful not only for curriculum planning and development but also for school administration.

The behavior of the people of Malitbog can be understood only with reference to their cultural orientation. It is within this orientation that children grow up and are trained. From childhood, for example, Malitbog children are taught what they need to know about locally desirable habits, attitudes, values, and modes of response, including the terms to use in identifying objects or in speaking to or about specific persons. Every adult farmer unceasingly and patiently works this out with the child so that by the time he is grown up, he has internalized the nuances of his culture which constitute his guide for social actions. In the process, he is not merely told about Malitbog norms and values but is required to carry them out in actual behavior. He is rewarded if he observes them and punished if he does not. These experiences are reinforced as the child matures. In spite of formal instruction in school, the behavior and outlook of the people of Malitbog remains consistent with the character and limitations of their traditional culture.

The relationship of knowledge and skills learned in school and those learned outside school behooves educators "to look beyond the schools and the people in them to the cultural context of education, in order to understand the problems and aspirations of education" (Spindler 1959:149). I hope this book contributes to stimulating further awareness of this relationship.

1 / The setting

THE PHILIPPINES consists of about 7100 islands and islets which dot the East China sea between Formosa and Indonesia. Topographically, most of these are hilly and mountainous in the interior and many are too rocky and barren for habitation. Seventy percent of the total land area is found in two big islands—Luzon and Mindanao. The 1960 census places the population of the entire country at 27 million.

Geographically, the Philippines is divided into three regions: Luzon, Bisayas, and Mindanao. The Bisayas constitute the central region of the country and include the islands lying between Luzon and Mindanao. These islands are Samar, Leyte, Bohol, Cebu, Siquijor, Negros, Panay, Masbate, Tablas, Sibuyan, Guimaras, and other smaller adjacent ones. The islands of Mindoro and Palawan are officially grouped under Luzon, in spite of their geographical location.

The inhabitants of these central islands are known as Bisayans. Although geographical conditions have set these different islands apart, the Bisayans share many social and cultural traits in common. Linguistically, however, they may be divided into eastern, central, and western Bisayans. The eastern Bisayans speak *Waray·waray,* the central group speak *Cebuano,* and the western people speak *Hiligaynon, Kiniray?a,* and *Aklanon.*[1] Morphologically, these languages belong to the Philippine subgroup of the Malayo-Polynesian linguistic family.

Panay island, the largest in western Bisayas, is almost an equilateral triangle, measuring approximately 169, 169, and 126.75 kilometers on the sides. It has an area of 11,520 square kilometers. A chain of mountains extends in a curved line from the northern to the southern points of the island, which joins at the middle another chain of low ridges, which runs toward the northeast, dividing the island into three parts. The southeastern part of Panay is occupied by the province of Iloilo. It is about 170 kilometers long and 60 kilometers wide, with a total land area of 5304.5 square kilometers. The northern part is occupied by the provinces of Aklan and Capiz, covering an area of 4410.1 square kilometers. The province of Antique embraces an area of 2679.3 square kilometers of narrow mountain slopes and deep valleys, stretching along the entire western coast of the island.

---

[1] The transcription used here for native terms is similar to that of the (Philippine) Institute of National Language orthography, except for the additional vowel /ə/ and the indication of glottal stop /?/. The lowering of /i/ and /u/ in final syllables is indicated by additional words *e* and *o,* respectively. Initial letters are capitalized according to the general practice in written English. A tentative phonemic analysis of *Kiniray?a* indicates the following segmental phonemes: /i a u ə p t k ? b d g m n ŋ l r s h y w/.

THE BARRIO

Malitbog (a pseudonym) is one of the small communities located in the central region of the island of Panay and near the political boundary line that separates the provinces of Capiz and Iloilo. Topographically, it is never broad at any point; it consists mainly of highlands, rolling hills, and shallow valleys. Five streamlets cut across the heart of the barrio from the highlands of Capiz to the plains of Iloilo, where they converge to form the Malitbog brook (see map). Deep run-offs taper from the hills to the banks of these streamlets, giving the area a checkered look from a distance. The upper portion of the community is steeper and cooler, while the lower section is somewhat warmer with abundant rain and green vegetation.

The intermediate location of the barrio between tall mountains and the plains gives it a healthful climate, characterized by abundant rain, relatively uniform humidity and gentle winds. Rains normally fall from 170 to 208 days a year, with an annual mean precipitation of 97.1 inches. Variations do occur; rainfall may be more or less than twice the normal precipitation in any month of the wet season which starts in June. The dry season begins in January, lasting for six months, although rains may come in February or in May. At any rate, local temperature is never extreme in either dry or wet season.

In spite of contacts with the outside world, especially with the *poblacion*[2] life, Malitbog has remained traditional. Communication is still a major problem. There are no roads to link the barrio with nearby towns or communities. What might be nearest to a road system is the rugged, narrow trail which connects it to the national road about 5 kilometers away. Transportation is largely a sled-and-carabao affair. Products are hauled to the road either on drawn sleds or over carabao backs, from where these are in turn brought to market by trucks or passenger buses. Sometimes men carry their loads on their heads, shoulders and backs. Often they attach these loads to both ends of a piece of bamboo which they carry across their shoulders, a method locally known as *tuwang·tuwang*.

Newspapers and magazines seldom reach the barrio. Two popular vernacular magazines which occasionally find their way into the hands of the farmers are the *Hiligaynon* and the *Yuhum*, published in Manila and Iloilo city, respectively. These materials are read more for short stories, serialized novels, and comic strips than for news. Transistorized radios have reached the barrio, but their possession is limited to a few who can afford them; hence, it will take some time before these can become an effective link between Malitbog and the outside world.

Mail is infrequent and letters, instead of being delivered by postal personnel, have to be picked by the addressee(s) or by friends at the municipal building during market days. In cases of first class or special delivery mails, the postman, through the town policeman, requests any Malitbog residents who may be in town to inform the addressee(s) to call for them. Privacy of communication is unknown; again and again my letters have been opened before being delivered to me. When I complained about it, my hosts were surprised at my "selfishness" by keeping

---

[2] The center of the town where the market, the church, the school, and the local government offices are found.

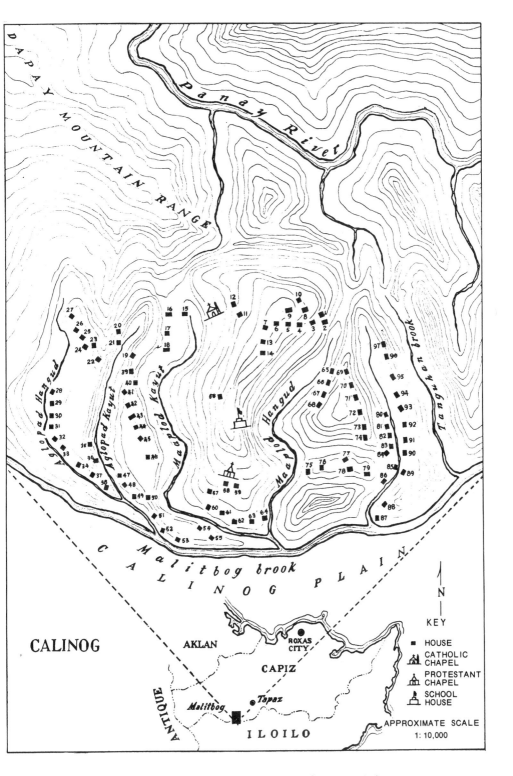

Malitbog settlement pattern. (Noel Escultura—1967)

"things" to myself. I found out later that it is part of the local expectation pattern to share with everyone any news coming from the outside; letters from friends and kin are normally circulated for everyone to read.

There is no electricity in the barrio, although the construction of a multimillion-peso hydroelectric plant at the headwaters of the nearby Jalaur River has already been planned. Lighting is supplied by kerosene lamps which are either homemade or purchased from Chinese stores in the town. At night, people carry torches or lanterns to light their way through narrow, slippery ridges. Some use battery-operated flashlights.

THE PEOPLE

Malitbog's population consists of about 1000 subsistence farmers. This number represents the total membership of 97 households scattered all over the barrio. Each family unit counts from six to ten members, mostly children, on the average. The relatively large number of children is partly explained by the belief that children are heavensent gifts, a grace from God, whose arrival, therefore, must not be controlled or interferred with; to do so is to commit a mortal sin. It is also explained in a more practical way with the saying that children are an economic investment; the more children one has the more one has upon which one can depend upon retirement from hard work. This explanation is supported by the local belief that every child, when grown up, means an extra farmhand, who will contribute to the family larder. Ironically, however, many Malitbog youths are out of the barrio in search of employment; those who stay marry young and establish their own families, independently of their parents.

The people of Malitbog, as a group, are very sensitive about their barrio. They would rather have anyone from within the community criticize it than hear a comment from an outsider. To them the barrio is the whole world, the entire Philippine society; since it is here that their immediate needs are met—it is here where they were born, married, and perhaps will be buried when they die. Thus, although internal differences may exist among them, the farmers usually act in concert whenever the whole barrio is threatened from the outside. The people's sensitivity is only matched by the manner in which they rate themselves in comparison with those living in the neighboring communities. The residents of the adjacent barrio of Kawayan, for example, are regarded by them as a "bunch of quick hands." Anything of value—such as water buffalo, pigs, chickens, or goats—lost in Malitbog is first searched for in Kawayan before attempts are made to look for it elsewhere. Every newcomer is likewise sized up as to character in terms of his place of origin.

This attitude toward outsiders illustrates how the people of Malitbog conceive of themselves and regard nonmembers of their barrio. In effect, it implies the existence of a stable social system woven around their belief that everyone stands in close relations with each other and therefore is quite distinct and apart from those who are nonmembers. This is reinforced by local myths which describe the people in the barrio as having common ancestors—Laki and Bayi. The couple had two children Bagit and Punay who, with no one to marry, took each other and bore Dumaraog.

Dumaraog took an unknown wife who bore him: Berhinu, Martin, and Luisa. From these siblings came the generations of Malitbog farmers.

Reference to these mythical ancestors, as a base in establishing affinity with a common tradition and with the community, is strengthened by local definition of group membership in terms of ecological orientation. By ecological definition of group membership is meant the manner in which a group of people perceive of themselves differently from others by utilizing the geographical location and social boundaries of their place of residence as points of reference. Malitbog is divided into three sitios: Agsiw, where most residents are *pangayaw* or emigrants to the place; Maʔaplod, where the inhabitants are *tumandok* or native to the place; and Aglupad, where the farmers are of mixed origin, that is, they are either native or emigrant to the place. These three sitios are not independent social or political units; they are merely subsections of the barrio. Local attachments to each sitio-residence, however, are strong and among themselves the people are known as *tiga*-Agsiw (meaning, from Agsiw), "*tiga*-Maʔaplod" and so on.

Every event in these sitios is regarded as a common enterprise and everybody is free to comment upon it. In fact no one can transact business with anybody without three or four individuals passing judgments over the deal. This sharing of intimate experiences develops into what Durkheim has called collective or common conscience, for as soon as a consensus among the people is formed and a norm is established, society lays down the appropriate rules for conduct, invested with corresponding moral authority for reward and punishment. Thus criticisms of any action or organization of group activities in a sitio are not made by an individual or certain groups of individuals, but by the entire sitio. This gives rise to a strong public opinion. Any misdemeanor is publicly censured and any slight eccentricity on the part of any person is given a *bansag* (nickname), which soon becomes generally known.

Internally therefore the sitio may be defined as a spatial and social unit within the broader geographical dimension of the barrio. Its boundaries are sociologically well defined. Insofar as the members are concerned, it is the locality in which they live; it is to them the "entire Malitbog," for within it the greater part of their life is spent. Here most of their basic needs are met because it is here where most of their close relatives and friends reside. The focal point of social interactions in the sitio is the coconut grove where the *tuba*[3] gatherer plies his trade. Here the men congregate on evenings and talk (while drinking) about community affairs; stores which can provide a common place for social gatherings being nonexistent. The barrio chapel is about the only place where most people come together during Sundays, but activities here have religious overtones.

Because of proximity to each other, only residents of a sitio are often involved in group activities like preparations for religious festivities, baptismal parties, wakes for the dead, and others. Residents of neighboring sitios may come, but they are regarded as guests. During barrio affairs, like the barrio fiesta, sitiomates crowd together and separate from those from other sitios. The same grouping pattern obtains among the young people during ball games, dances, *bilasyon* (wake for the dead), and group meetings. In fact, one source of trouble at the affairs in the *baylihan*

---

[3] Local wine derived from treated sap of freshly cut coconut flowers.

Cluster of houses in one of the higher sections of Malitbog.

Malitbog couple working in the field. Usually, the wife helps the husband in preparing the field for planting.

(improvised dance halls) during occasions is dancing with a girl from another sitio without first seeking permission from her sitiomate male chaperon.

Labor for building a house, agricultural pursuits, mending fences, and other work activities is recruited from sitio members. Collection of barrio contributions to the annual town fiesta is based upon the size of a sitio; each sitio is held responsible for meeting its fiscal obligations. Membership in the barrio council is also drawn from the three sitios.

MATERIAL CULTURE

Malitbog houses are found in clusters situated along narrow trails on top of ridges adjacent to the farms. Houses in each cluster range from 2 to 12. The standard house type is a square, four-walled, one-to-two-room house with triangularly shaped roofs made of dried leaves of grass, locally known as *cogon*. It is generally raised above the ground on bamboo or timber posts; props called *sulay* support the older houses from all sides.

Access to the house is through bamboo stairs pegged to the threshold of the door. Certain beliefs are associated with constructing doors, stairs, and windows which the people carefully observe. Stairs, for example, must always have odd steps, preferably seven because even numbers bring bad luck; doors and at least one or two windows should be constructed at the east side of the house, or early death would come to one of the occupants.

Most Malitbog houses are furnished with bamboo chairs and tables. However, the family eats on the floor, because tables are normally reserved for guests. Spoons and glasses are also reserved for visitors; the members of the family eat with their fingers and drink from clean coconut shells. Rice is emptied from the pot into woven trays called *tubu?* and vegetables into tin plates called *sartin;* the china is kept for special occasions.

As in other parts of Panay, dress and ornaments are important exterior manifestations of social status. However, these are rarely the topic of discussion and gossip because most of the people except four families are in about the same economic class. Anyone with a new dress or shirt is indeed admired, but it would not be correct to say that to be well dressed is the explicit ambition of all villagers.

Older women wear *patadyong* (barrel skirts) purchased from traveling merchants or from dealers in town during market days. Weaving is a municipal specialization in Panay. Towns noted for barrel skirts are Tigbawan, Miagao, and San Joaquin in Iloilo province. The people themselves in Malitbog no longer weave their own clothing; their attire is of commercial cotton. A long time ago, some informants say, the people wove fabrics derived from palm leaves and abaca fibers; today abaca fibers are stripped mainly for making ropes, and palm leaves are no longer utilized.

In planting or harvesting seasons, the women wear a dress with long sleeves as protection from the heat of the sun and from sharp leaves of grass. However, dresses similar to those worn by women in the *poblacion* are used during nonworking days. On special occasions they apply cosmetics on their lips and darken their eyebrows with eyebrow pencils. They also powder their faces and drench the collars of their dress with perfume. The older, married women, however, do not groom as much; they simply don clean attire. They do not use any cosmetics because they would be branded as "flirts" if they did and would certainly be shamed in public by their husbands.

The men wear short pants while working in the fields. Often, they do not wear shirts (which they reserve for special occasions) and thus they work half naked. During special occasions, they don long pants and well-pressed shirts, smooth their hair with pomade, and use some perfume. Young men wear shoes only during special affairs and generally go about the barrio barefooted. Men wear their hair short and usually get it trimmed every two weeks by the local barber.

Few people in the barrio have watches. Anyhow, it is not deemed important because time is told by a rapid glance at the sun and there is no need to know the exact hour. The time, as the farmers know it, follows the position of the sun, the nature of work schedules, and the movements of birds and domestic animals.

ECONOMIC SUBSISTENCE

The mainstay of economic life in Malitbog is wet-rice agriculture, although dry or upland rice is also planted on the hillsides. In narrow valleys and plains, dikes are built to catch rainfall and crude terracing is done in lower hills for similar purpose. Planting starts in May for upland rice and in June and July for the lowland variety. The use of the plow and carabao, reinforced by magic and prayer to insure successful harvest, characterizes the agricultural technology of the area.

The first plowing of the field for upland rice starts early in March. The hot sun of April dries and kills the grass, and when the second plowing is done, as soon as rain comes in May, the field is practically clean. Planting is done by broadcasting the seeds. For lowland cultivation, plowing starts in April and continues to early May. Planting involves sowing the seeds over a prepared seedbed and transplanting the seedlings when they are about one-foot high. Rituals, prayers, and other forms of ceremonialism are performed to hasten growth of the rice, ward off the evil spirits from the field, and insure a good harvest. The observance of these rituals follows the agricultural cycle.

Aside from rice, the farmers also plant sweet potatoes, beans, and other crops and vegetables either for family consumption or for market purposes. In cultivating sweet potatoes, the farmer also performs a number of rituals and observes certain natural phenomena. For example, the night before he plants his crops he observes the sky. If there are many stars he proceeds to plant the following morning, but if the sky is dark and cloudy, he postpones the activity until a favorable day comes. In planting *cassava,* an edible root crop used as supplementary staple during lean months, the farmer spreads out his fingers before putting the cuttings into the ground in order to insure strong and well-distributed roots. He is also careful not to invert the cuttings—that is, upside down, because, according to the existing belief, this would make the starchy roots of the crop highly poisonous.

Field products are supplemented by some fishing. Freshwater fish, locally known as *haru?an, pantat,* and *tilapia,* are caught by traps, fishhooks, and by draining

Pulling weeds from the rice field is a woman's job. To protect themselves from the heat of the sun, the girls don dresses with long sleeves and bandanas similar to the one worn by the girl in the photo.

water from rice paddies, an activity known as *sag?a*. Mud shells, known as *?ige,* are gathered from September through December. These are either sold in the town or used for family consumption. Ricebirds are the only game hunted in the area.

RELIGION

Like any other Philippine barrio, Malitbog has not escaped Christian influences. Two types of Christian orientations exist in the barrio—Roman Catholicism and Protestantism. Catholicism was brought to Panay by the Spaniards as early as the late-sixteenth century. However, its impact was not felt in the central area, where Malitbog is located, until 1763 when the pueblo of Calinog was founded. The religious center in Calinog then was a *bisita* (Sp. *visita*) under the parochial jurisdiction of the neighboring town of Passi. With the establishment of Calinog as a town in 1810, the *bisita* was elevated to an independent parish and more converts to Roman Catholicism were gained. The use of force, especially during the building of the church, was not lacking to bring the people under the influence of the new faith. Preaching was normally an attack against the "sinful" ways of the people. The fear of hell and the promise of eternal life in heaven were among the incentives used to attract people to the new religion.

Cruelty on the part of the later Spanish friars and of local authorities of Calinog forced many families to leave the *poblacion* for the frontier area near the present site of Malitbog, where they settled. Their contacts with the *poblacion* people became infrequent; many went to the town only for certain household necessities or to visit their relatives during fiestas.

The founding of the parish of Tapaz in 1844 strengthened the position of Roman Catholicism in the area, drawing more people into the fold of the Church. When the Americans came in 1900, further changes took place. The construction of the national road connecting the provinces of Capiz and Iloilo improved transportation in the area; more Catholic residents came and this resulted in the further spread of the new religion.

An event that was later to become important to Malitbog was the sending in 1930 by the Baptist Foreign Mission, stationed in Jaro, Iloilo city, of a minister to establish a rural church in this frontier area. In those days, houses were scattered throughout the area, often near the hillsides where the people had their swidden patches.[4] With the construction of the chapel in 1931, the minister was able to persuade the farmers to live in one place and to organize themselves into a barrio. Seminary students from a mission school in Iloilo city visited Malitbog regularly during holidays and semestral vacations and intensified religious activities in the area.

Protestantism was widespread in the area at the outbreak of World War II in 1941. By 1955 the barrio was about 85% Protestant, and by 1960 the Protestant converts far exceeded the Roman Catholics. In this year a new wood-and-concrete Protestant church with galvanized-iron roof was constructed.

---

[4] A small clearing planted to rice and rootcrops. This system of farming involves slashing and burning the forest or any mature vegetation before planting.

Upon my return to Malitbog in 1964, I noted remarkable changes in the religious orientation of the people. A number of families had withdrawn their membership from the Protestant church, while others remained Protestant, but were not active in church work. Many re-embraced Roman Catholicism. Many elders of both churches had recourse to mediums and herb-medicine practitioners for their illnesses, spiritual needs, and emotional problems.

This recourse to local practices suggests that in spite of outward manifestation of adherence to Christianity, traditional religion still plays a significant role in the lives of the people. Many local activities associated with planting, harvesting, and storing of crops, building houses, treating the sick, and getting married are based on popular beliefs sanctioned by the local culture but not necessarily by either the Catholic or Protestant religion. Thus upon the vaguely defined concept of Christianity, a highly specialized knowledge concerning the *ʔingkantu* (environmental spirits) and other supernatural beings is superimposed. In fact, Roman Catholic saints are often revered, not because the Church has canonized them for their sacrifices and virtuous living, but because they possess powers similar to those of the *ʔingkantu* and can be manipulated for personal ends.

Viewed in the light of this thinking, the introduction of Christianity appears not to have led to any significant shift in the emphasis placed on folk belief, attitudes, and practices. The traditional system of ethics in the barrio, particularly within the sphere of human-superhuman relationships, remains deeply embedded in the local culture, and even at the popular level of thought, the numerous sayings, legends, and ritual observances have a strong effect upon the general system of morality. Even exposure to suburban life in the town, on account of trading and going to church on Sundays, has not reduced the significance of local ceremonialism with regard to agricultural, technological, and social activities in the barrio.

2 / The child in Malitbog society

MUCH OF WHAT A PERSON DOES OR THINKS as an adult member of society is learned through socialization which begins at birth. To gain a better understanding of this process it is imperative to know first how Malitbog society anticipates the coming of the child, childhood being the base line of learning and transmission of culture. Moreover, the social and cultural environment, mediated through the family, constitutes the antecedent condition which influences the training of children and, consequently, the behavior of the adults.

ADULTS' VIEW OF THE CHILD

In Malitbog, children are much desired and enjoyed. Adults fondle children whenever possible, and one hears fathers sing in the middle of the night in order to pacify crying children. During the day, the shrill voice of a mother or of a female sibling rocking a child to sleep is a familiar sound. Malitbog adults apparently never tire of children. A weary father would rather forego his much needed noonday nap than brush aside a child who comes to play with him. A busy laborer would leave his pressing task to fix a child's toy, to tease him, or to pick him up for a kiss. Parents and siblings are scolded by the older folks if they neglect to attend immediately to a crying child, crying being considered bad for children. Even during important affairs like religious seances, children are given much freedom to do as they please. I have watched Inggo, a medium, stop chanting a number of times during an important religious performance to pick up a child which kept disarranging his ritual paraphernalia and, without a word, put it down at a distant corner. The mother simply told the child not to do it again; the older folks giggled amusedly.

Of course extremely naughty children are not spared the rod. Everyone agrees that children are children and must be disciplined while young. However, most parents are quite permissive with children and punish them only as a last recourse. Children are often considered to be the joy of the home. Informants admit that "these young creatures shake the house with their noise—romping up and down, shouting, crying, and fighting," but, as one father said, "the house becomes so lonely without them; it is as though someone has passed away." This man's wife and children were away for two weeks when I interviewed him. Almost all the parents I talked to expressed the view that they wanted to have more children; they argued in practical terms: "Children are some kind of investment. When you grow old you can be sure someone will take care of you; there is always a secure place to stay."

Other reasons for wanting more children have supernatural undertones. For example, children are considered gifts of God, the grace derived from divine blessings, the result of clean, honest living. Clean life is described as "entering into matrimony with parental consent; the woman must be chaste and the man must have had no illicit love affairs before marriage." Infringement of this traditional norm brings about bad luck to either of the spouses. Sterility on the part of the woman and impotence on the part of the man are among the severe supernatural punishments for such trespasses; unacceptable behavior like eloping in protest against parental wishes, cursing God or parents for any personal disappointments, or making fun of couples without children are likewise dealt with accordingly. These censures surrounding the coming of children make the child central to any marriage, and the desire to have more children a religious and social requirement, because the birth of a child is a public testimony that the parents have led clean, obedient, and pious lives during their prenuptial and through their child-bearing days. Seen from this perspective, it is understandable that the arrival of a child is a welcomed event in Malitbog.

Because children are supposed to be gifts of God, infants are considered to be "sweet, clean, spotless, and pure" little angels whose neglect brings about unbearable misfortunes to the entire family. This view would seem to contradict the concensus among informants that everyone is born in original sin. Nevertheless, parents who do not welcome the arrival of a child or who deprive it of the necessary adult attention and care are punished—they either suffer from a lingering illness or from a hard economic life. That is why birth control has never been popular in the barrio; the majority of the people frown upon the practice.

Newborn babies fall in two categories: the baptized and the unbaptized. The unbaptized are considered half-human, their popular nickname being *muritu* (not yet human). Such babies are viewed as constitutionally weak and are susceptible to illness. They do not yet enjoy the protective concern of their guardian angels. Should they die, their souls cannot enter heaven; instead, they would be turned into environmental spirits, the *tomawu* (a generic term for dwellers of the trees) and sent back to haunt the living. Some Catholic informants further opined that before becoming environmental spirits, the souls of unbaptized children stay in *limbo,* a dark place located in a region between the earth and the sky adjacent to *purgatoryo.* The length of stay in this place depends upon the seriousness of the original sin inherited from the parents. This world view shows how Christian concepts are modified to suit local ways of thinking and believing.

Baptized children are called *Santo Anhil* (Saint Angels). They are considered physically strong and relatively free from the wiles of the surrounding spirits. Their guardian angels are believed to be in constant watch over them. Most parents do not show much concern over the death of baptized children, because God will take care of them in heaven. This does not mean that they love the unbaptized more, but that they are assured they have not committed a mortal sin; they have done their part in preparing the child for its heavenly abode. If a child's baptism has not yet been followed by a *compirma* (that is, the sacrament of confirmation), the people believe that upon its demise the soul will have to pass purgatory first in order to atone for some of its original sin. However, if the *compirma* has been performed, the soul will go directly to heaven, there to be received by the singing cherubims. This is one reason why mourning upon the death of a child is discouraged; the bereaved parents are cajoled not to grieve so much because the "angels in heaven are taking care of it; your tears will only add more burden to yourselves."

Another widespread concept in the barrio is the belief that behavior is genetically inherited. Everyone is said to be born with specific traits already structured for him and he seldom can do anything about them. A popular proverb cryptically states this view: "*ʔang batasan nasa duguʔka tawo* [behavior (or habits) is in the blood of a person; it is in the veins]." Another frequently quoted saying reinforces this concept: "*Kun anuʔ ʔang punuʔ ʔamu man ʔang bunga* [whatever is the tree, so shall be its fruits]." Thus a good child is proof that the parents are honest and morally upright; they do not have bad traits in their veins. The bad child is an evidence to the contrary. A child born with undesirable traits will always be *bad* no matter how hard the parents try to discipline him; no amount of education can reform him either. It is his fate to be born that way. As one doting mother said: "What can I do? My son is born with these traits—his actions are beyond his control."

A good child is quiet, obedient, and respectful. He keeps out of trouble; he is industrious and generous. He does not roam around the barrio with other children, but stays home and helps in the domestic chores, takes care of other siblings, and does other useful jobs. A good child, by local standards, is one who meets all or a greater number of community norms and values of social behavior.

BIRTH CONTROL

Because children are wanted, birth control is, as has already been pointed out, not popular in Malitbog. It is practiced, however, by educated Protestant couples and sickly mothers, who use either local preventives (that is, herbals) or the modern techniques learned from the missionaries. Massaging the womb out of its place, known as *batak ka matris* (to pull back the womb), is one of the traditional ways of controlling birth. It is believed that by doing this the *tinʔe* (intestine, though what is actually referred to here is the birth canal) will be out of place, thus preventing pregnancy. Not everyone can do the *batak ka matris;* it takes a specialist to do it. The use of abortives is not popular, although they are used by some women. *Balungay* (a kind of tree with tiny leaves used for vegetables) leaves are pounded, heated, and poulticed around the abdomen of a woman. A decoction of the bark of another medicinal plant known as *bitaʔ* is taken internally. The bitterness of the bark and the heat from the poultice, it is said, dissolve the fetus inside the womb. This is known as *hulug*. The *partira* (midwife) refused to tell me the names of the other plants used for abortion for fear of losing her skill.

Devout Catholics in the barrio cannot understand why "the good seed of man" should be wasted "by preventing it from bringing forth the gift of God." They regard the traditional housewives who practice abortion and the educated ones who practice natural (the rhythm) method of birth control as sinners. Many are sure that these women "will certainly go to hell." As one informant summarized the consensus of opinion in the area:

> When these women die, they will be brought before our Lord who will ask: "Why did you kill your child?" And what will they say? Surely, they cannot tell lies because God can see through our hearts, He knows what we humans are doing. If our hearts are black, as these women's, God will certainly say: "You have murdered an innocent child; you have rejected my gift. Go and burn in hell for all the mortal sins you have committed in my name."

Hell is conceived as a place located underneath the bowels of the earth, characterized by the presence of eternal fire and big snakes that strangle the souls upon their arrival. Then the struggling souls are dragged deep into the burning pit. This image has crystallized in the minds of the people of Malitbog through reproductions of medieval paintings they have seen hanging on the walls of the Catholic church in town, depicting various scenes in hell. Demons, known as *yawaʔ* and evil spirits live in this place of fire.

Souls of fetuses "killed" by abortion are brought by the angels to a dark place somewhere; nobody knows its exact location. This place is not the same as *limbo* because the victims are not yet humans; they have not breathed the air of life on earth. The crying of these souls often angers the angels, who punish the erring mothers with sterility, illness, misfortunes, and eternal damnation in hell when they die. By way of showing that mothers who practice birth control are punished, the barrio folk wil say: "Look at those who practice that 'control, control'—they are hard up in life; others are sickly."

As already stated, scientific birth control was introduced by the Protestant missionaries in 1953. It does not, however, involve oral contraceptives, as only the rhythm method is used. Five couples have practiced this method. One housewife has not conceived for five years, the other for eight years, and another for nine years. This is shown by the following tabulation:

Mothers	Number of Children	Age of Last Child	Length of Practice in Years
A	5	8	8
B	6	5	4
C	2	3	3
D	1	2	2½
E	4	6	5
F	2	12	9

One couple admitted practicing *coitus interruptus* before they were introduced to the "more satisfying rhythm method." In my field notes appear the following entry of an interview with a female informant.

> *February 12, 1964.* Early this morning, Bien, wife of Sam, came to my boarding house and after a preliminary talk about children and their economic implications for married life, volunteered to talk about sexual intercourse and about birth control. In the past, I had a hard time prodding informants to talk about this subject matter. Bien frankly discussed it with me and with those present in the

house. She said that before the coming of the Protestant missionaries in Malitbog she and her husband practiced *coitus interruptus* as a means of preventing pregnancy.

"You see Mr. Ukano, I come from a very prolific family," she explained, "and so does my husband. But we are too poor to afford many children. So we talked the matter over for a long time and decided to control my childbirths, which were then annual."

I reminded her that according to some people controlling is a sin. "I think it is more sinful to have more children and be unable to support them," Bien argued. "Beside I pity my husband who works so hard in order to provide for a family which is getting bigger and bigger each year. So for a while my husband and I did not sleep together. But we found it rather difficult to keep suppressing one's desires.

"One night we tried the withdrawal method. It was alright at first. But as weeks went by, something strange began to take place. We were both unsatisfied with it. I became irritable and so did my husband. I was restless. I felt like wanting to have some more food when I could not have it—you seem to be hanging in the air. That was what drove us crazy—my husband and myself— and we always quarreled.

"Then one day a lady missionary came to our church. She gathered a number of us married women and explained how one could overcome the problem. You see, I asked her about it. She said that with this new method "one can control childbirth and enjoy sexual relations." She gave me a small calendar, saying that "a woman is not fertile seven days after menstruation and five days before. All you have to do is mark the beginning and end of your monthly cycles. I followed her instruction and it was really satisfying."

"The new method is good, but my poor husband has to wait for a long time. Sometimes he complains," Bien further explained.

While Bien said she is practicing the new method, she also observes the traditional *libe* (prohibitions) which the old folk use to prevent pregnancy. She drinks herb concoction. When I pressed for names of the plants she uses, she refused to tell.

"Are there many women who are following your examples?" I asked.

"So far there are only five of us," she answered. "But I hope many more will follow in the future."

"What do other people say about your new techniques of controlling birth?"

"We are not considered good women; we are sinners and will surely go to hell," she laughed.

The other form of birth control is abstinence. The people I talked to agreed that "abstinence has its emotional inconveniences, but it is the safest way to control birth without committing sin." Osing, for example, purposely followed seasonal labor in other regions of Panay island to be away from his wife. "How do you manage your sex life?" I asked him casually one day. He smiled and said:

Very well. Sometimes I am too tired to think about sex; even if I desire it, it is physically impossible. I am afraid I cannot afford a big family and this is one reason why I often want to stay away from my wife. Sometimes I reason to myself, "Well—why do I keep doing this? If it is God's wish that we have more children, He will find a way for me to support them." Then I will become bold. But when I come to think about the consequence of giving everything to God I am afraid; I am afraid of having more children than I can support.

Many other informants say that abstinence is difficult to follow religiously in that "you need your wife beside you, don't you? You must keep her there or else she looks for another man." One farmer jokingly explained why it is difficult to suppress male sexual urges in this manner. "There is no other form of entertainment that can keep our minds off from sex, especially at night. We go to bed early and once we are near our wives we forget that we are not supposed to have some more babies." This opinion is not shared by many because evening visits and serenading are still fashionable among the men. Nevertheless, this statement sheds light on the problem of birth control and the attendant inability of the people to pace the coming of children. Masturbation is an outlet of sexual release most husbands admit, but some are afraid to try it because "it is said to be bad for the health."

While a birth control problem exists among some people in Malitbog, the desire for children is also present in others. There are ten couples in the barrio who do not have children. Sterile women are known as *namarhan* (had dried up). Sterility is caused by abnormal menstruation, prolonged sickness, and old age. Tio C. smiled when I asked him why some women are sterile saying, "A woman who remains unmarried for a long time is likely to dry up." Impotence is due to a man's having only one testicle (*?itlog*). Such a man is known as *?abil,* a condition that is either congenital or acquired as a punishment by the supernatural beings for his wanton premarital sexual excesses. Riding on the warm back of a carabao and sitting on objects long exposed to the heat of the sun cause impotence, although the circumstances surrounding these acts are controlled by the supernatural beings. The curse (*sumpa?*) of disappointed parents, older kinsmen, or victimized virgins also causes impotence.

A barren couple is called *baw?as.* Sometimes people say that "their bloods are not compatible." Any medication which may be tried is seldom effective. Prayers to certain saints are said to be more efficacious in correcting the malfunctioning of the body in bearing children. Pilgrimages to known miraculous churches and places in the island of Panay, such as the town of Leganes near Iloilo city, and keeping yearly vows to favorite patron saints, are means of curing impotence and sterility.

3 / Pregnancy and birth

THE PEOPLE OF MALITBOG see human life as a pattern of continuous and irreversible stages of growth and development. Each stage in this progression is different from all other stages; each requires different biological and intellectual capacities for social participation in group life. Some believe that the process starts during pregnancy, but most contend that it starts immediately at conception —the period when actual mother and child relations begin. To support this latter view, the people point to the fact that any physical or emotional strain on the part of the mother affects the development of the fetus. For example, unsatisfied cravings for certain foods may cause abortion, excessive manual work like laundering, or planting rice may cause miscarriage; and unnecessary worry may result in congenital defects.

Because of the belief that any disruption of the prenatal relationship between the mother and the child will unduly affect the latter's adaptability to extrauterine life, conception, pregnancy, and birth are surrounded with a body of *libe* (prohibitions) and ceremonialism. These range from the simple notation of omens during conception to the elaborate rites observed during difficult delivery. They are intended to protect both the mother and the child from the hazards of the natural environment and the "evil designs" of the supernatural beings, especially the malevolent spirits. Since growth is viewed as beginning at conception, it is logical to start descriptive analysis of the process from this stage.

CAUSES OF PREGNANCY

The people believe that pregnancy is the result of two major causes: the *natural cause,* which involves physical contact between a man and a woman, and the *supernatural cause,* which is brought about by some unknown power. The natural cause is in reality sexual intercourse (*ʔiyot*). It is through this act that the *təɾəs* (generic term for male sperm and the female ovum) of the man unites with that of the woman, forming a child. The *təɾəs* is conceived as *duguʔ nga sinaɾaʔ* (distilled human blood). This is one reason why the people maintain that "blood is thicker than water."

Pregnancy due to supernatural cause involves coitus between an environmental spirit and a woman, with the latter hardly knowing it. Even if aware of it, she could

20

not refuse the act for, as one informant stressed, "Who could stop the spirits from doing what they like?" Some victims are said to have been informed about the coitus through a dream, confirmed by a wet vaginal area; others "know about it only after their menses stop and their bellies start to bulge."

For a man to impregnate a woman there must be repeated coitus. Once or twice is not believed to be enough to cause conception. As Mal?am Miguel, a carpenter, puts it: "If it takes several weeks to complete a simple house, so, I imagine it would take several unions to form a human being." Sexual intercourse is bad when done during the day; the environmental spirits might chance to witness the act and the baby will have physical deformity.

The men initiate the sexual act because "it is not proper for any woman to do so." Many couples I have talked to agreed that "only bad women initiate sexual relations." As one of the elderly women puts it, "The husband will suspect the morals of his wife if she makes the first move. So the women simply wait. Anyway, no man can lie beside a woman without doing what he thinks is to be done."

Conversation and preliminary love play seldom form part of the sexual act in Malitbog. Male informants state, "You simply lie down beside your wife and do it. If you talk, the children might wake up or other people—especially your in-laws—might hear. It is embarrassing." The frequency of sexual intercourse ranges from one to three times a week. Late evenings or toward dawn is the most favored time.

CONCEPTION

The generic term for conception is *panamkən*. This is the natural outcome of sexual intercourse. Everybody expects that a woman must conceive a month after marriage. If no sign is noted, like the stopping of the menses or early morning sickness, the couple is chided for being "inefficient in their work." "*Dali? dali?a ninyo* [Hurry up]" the old folk tease them.

As soon as her menses stop, a woman is known as *nadəktan* and she announces this to her husband, close kin and friends, enthusiastically saying: "*Hoy, nadəktan dən ako* [Say, I have something already]". The husband is careful not to annoy her and, as Flor said, smiling, "It is the time to become spoiled." Of course no visible changes at this point appear, except a good appetite and a predisposition to sleep.

Nadəktan is followed by another phase characterized by a lack of appetite, morning nausea, and dizziness. Informants refer to this phase descriptively as the period of sickness. The young wife is now the object of open jokes from the older folks. Whenever she is met by them, they tease her, saying: "*?ano may malatiki? dən?* [Say, do you have a house lizard already?]". The fetus is likened to a house lizard because of the local belief that a child is born with a double in the form of a gecko. Thus, grandmothers and older members of the household always see to it that all pots are covered before the children are put to sleep. A double travels at night and should it fall into a crevice or a pot, the child would die of *hupa?* or bad dreams.

During conception, a woman is the object of supernatural attention. These non-humans, who always wish ill to conceiving mothers, cause nausea and morning sickness. Any comment from them about a woman's condition would make the woman sick. This is known as *nabugnohan*. To cure this illness a *luy?ahan* ritual is performed immediately after the attack. The rite is simple, varying from one healer to another. One such rite was performed by Elda, a midwife, in 1964, as follows:

Marya, a young bride of five months, suddenly suffered violent nausea and fever. Her husband, Berto, called Elda to attend to her. Everyone in the neighborhood also came, because Marya's mother became hysterical, wailing and shouting for help.

On arrival, Elda went directly to Marya without pausing and speaking to anyone. After feeling her pulse and forehead, she turned to Marya's mother and asked for a piece of ginger. She sliced one half of it into seven parts and simply peeled the other half. The seven slices were roasted, wrapped in a piece of cloth, and applied over the patient's pulse. She pressed the ginger with two fingers of her right hand, and prayed, announcing later the cause of the illness. She said Marya had exposed herself too much while taking a bath in the nearby spring, and the environmental spirits had noticed her, and commented about her not following the accepted taboos. Marya's sister confirmed the fact that indeed she and the patient had taken a bath at the nearby spring two days ago, and Marya did not cover herself modestly, for "It was noontime and we thought no one was within seeing distance." However, the spirits saw Marya, and this was the cause of her illness, the midwife explained.

After ascertaining the ailment, Elda threw the slices of ginger out of the window as she gave a sharp cry: "Haw!" She then pounded the other half of the peeled ginger with her hand, rubbed it over Marya's soles, palms of her hand, temples, forehead, and finally on the crown of her head. Meanwhile, she was murmuring her magic prayer. This done, she pressed the ginger hard against Marya's head and blew it three times, saying: "I call on you departed kin of this woman—please protect her from the evil spirits. Haw!" Then she removed the object and tied it to Marya's dress. True enough, Marya stopped vomiting!

Many informants agree that the *luy?ahan* ritual is effective. As one of them narrated:

> When I was pregnant with my first child I also suffered from a sudden attack of nausea and fever. There were times when I thought I would die. One day I brought food to my husband and on the way I had the attack. I thought that was the end of me. It was good that Karyo, son of Inggo, was tending his carabao nearby and when he saw me, he called for my husband. I was brought home and my mother performed the *luy?ahan*. Since that time I never had the attack.

During the period of conception, a craving for a certain food develops. The craving is said to be "unbearable" and the husband should procure the particular food or the wife becomes fretful the whole day. Abortion might also occur if the craving is not satisfied. It is said that the craving is dictated by the unborn child. This is known as *?ima*. "You see," explained Tia P., "the child also hungers for certain food as we grown-ups do. But since it is still inside the womb, it communicates through the mother."

Panamkan discomforts are not limited to mothers only. Some husbands admit that they too suffer from the same sickness as their wives. They also develop an uncontrollable desire for food and sleep; they suffer from morning sickness and nausea; and, likewise, they become emotionally disturbed. *Panamkən* fits are transferred to the husband by the wife's having "tripped" over him while he is asleep, an act known as *lakad*.

Because of the close connection between a mother and her child during this stage of development, whatever the mother eats influences the child's physical and emotional life. If the mother prefers coconut meat, the child will have a white complexion; if dark-colored fruits—like *duhat* or *lumbuy*—the child will also be dark skinned. Narrated one informant:

> When I was conceiving of my first boy, I took an intense like for *duhat* and *bagnay* [these are dark-peeled fruits]. My husband and I frequently quarreled because even if it were midnight and the craving came he had to go out to secure some fruits. You see, if I could not eat what I liked I lost consciousness. He used to tell me: "Oh, you are merely acting. You should be in the movies." But no— I could not explain why I felt that way; it simply happened. The feeling would be gone as soon as I have eaten what I liked. Everybody predicted I would give birth to a dark-skinned baby. I did not believe them then—but now, my Rudy is dark skinned, isn't he?

As well as food, persons and objects may sometimes affect a conceiving mother. Like food, intense admiration for persons or desire for certain objects may influence the physical appearance of the child.

> Caring was conceiving when the American missionaries [locally known as *Kanoʔ*] came to the barrio. She was attracted to one male missionary who sang very well. Of course she could not come near him because she was ashamed. So she kept her distance; nonetheless, she stared at him long and carefully. She admired his eyes, his hair, his nose, his voice, and his ways of walking. She had almost followed the missionary every day during the week that the group was in Malitbog. When she finally gave birth, the infant looked like the *Kanoʔ*.

If the desired food or object is not secured, the conceiving mother will become sick and a miscarriage will likely take place, unless treated right away. According to informants, this happened to Benita three years ago.

> Benita went out of the house to take her morning walk. She was conceiving of her second boy. A vendor with green mangoes passed by. Suddenly, Benita took a liking for mangoes; however, she did not have money to purchase one. She tried to borrow money but no one within the immediate neighborhood had money at that time. She did not tell the man she was conceiving. The following day Benita dropped to her knees unconscious as she stepped out of the house. She was very ill; two days later she gave birth to a dead fetus.

Because of the moral responsibility for refusing to give way to a conceiving woman, an unscrupulous individual in the barrio exploits the *panamkən* trait to justify his stealing a neighbor's choice jackfruit or banana, or haggling over the price of a trade item being peddled by a merchant or being displayed at the store in town. A woman, for example, would simply feign to be conceiving and a storekeeper merchant would give way to her desire, even if it would mean a loss of business. To deny a conceiving woman her desire is, in terms of local belief, to commit murder should the fetus die; it is a mortal sin, an eternal damnation in hell.

PRENATAL CARE

In her second or third month of pregnancy a woman is known as *nagadara* "because her belly is now visibly big, as though she is carrying something in her skirt." Many parents consider this period the most dangerous phase of pregnancy because the fetus "is now in human form and the spirits are more determined to harm it." A midwife is called for the necessary rituals and prenatal care.

Prenatal treatment is done at home. In a small house a room is improvised by partitioning the living room with a blanket or *?amakan* (mat made of bamboo splints put up across it). Windows and other big openings are closed in order to prevent malevolent spirits and *mala?in nga hangin* (evil winds) from getting in. The mother lies flat on her back; sometimes she is allowed to flex her legs. Sitting beside her, the midwife applies ginger on her soles, pulse, palms, forehead, temples, and crown of the head. As she does this, she prays, afterward massaging the belly of the woman—slowly and carefully from one side to the other.

From seven to nine months, a pregnant woman is known as *manugbata?* (about to deliver her child). This is the period when the sex of the child is predicted by friends and close relatives. If the weight and protrusion of the woman's belly lean toward the left, it is believed that her baby will be a girl; if to the right, it will be a boy. If she has shown marked temperament during conception, the baby will certainly be a boy; otherwise, it will be a girl. Most parents wish a son for their first-born; some mothers prefer a girl so they can have an "early helper at home."

CHILDBIRTH

Preparation   A woman is not allowed to stray away from her house on the approach of her date of delivery. If necessary, she goes out accompanied by a child or someone older. "Anything can happen to you now, that is why you have to bring Endring along," Tia P. reminded her pregnant daughter when she protested against the niece coming along to visit a relative two hills away. During this time, everybody is anxious about the coming of the baby and the welfare of the mother. Friends and relatives passing by inquire about the woman's definite confinement. Her mother and sisters prepare the things necessary for the event: old but clean clothes to be used as waistbands (*bigkis*); several barrel skirts; clean pieces of cloth made from soft materials with which to wrap the newly born baby, and, of course, the baby's clothes. Her grandmother, if living, prepares the *pangalap*. This consists of objects known to have powers to protect the mother from environmental spirits during the crucial hour of childbirth. This *pangalap* is normally passed from grandmother to granddaughter, although it can be mediated through the mother if the former is dead.

The men folk also have their share in the preparation. The husband secures coconut oil, clean coconut shells, a fat hen, a quantity of firewood, big pots, clean bamboo tubes for the placenta and blood, and water containers. The father of the woman builds the *?idagan* (delivery bed), although many contemporary young mothers refuse to use this furniture. An elderly woman in the neighborhood who had not had much difficulty in delivering or had not lost a child in the process (locally known as *matingas? et paminata?*) is called to assist in the delivery.

As soon as hard and frequent pain is felt by the expectant mother, a midwife is sent for, if one is not already staying with her. Close relatives and neighbors are also requested "to please come and help." The woman's mother or sister is notified if she is not living in the same house. This is because childbirth is one of the crucial events in the life of a woman; she is described as being at the portal of death. That is why everything is done to prevent the occurrence of any unfortunate event. Thus in calling for the midwife the husband is enjoined to observe a number of taboos. For example, he must not look back until he reaches the house of the midwife. Upon nearing the house he must call out loud three times and cup the newel of the stairs before entering the door. This is done so that the midwife cannot say no and the evil spirits cannot interfere with the trip. Many informants say that by this time the evil spirits are always on the lookout to "prevent the birth of the child." They may cause accidents which would prevent the midwife in assisting the mother. That is why all necessary and known measures have to be carried out carefully. If the midwife refuses to come, the husband must insist, and should carry her on his shoulder, if necessary.

Delivery   A woman is "ready" when her labor pains become steady and cramps are felt by her around her waistline. She is then made to lean against a pile of pillows supported behind by a *ba?ul* (trunk) or any hard object strong enough to brace her in a reclining position. Her legs are separated and stretched, with the feet resting on the foot brace. The purpose of the foot brace is to provide something on which the mother can push hard at the moment of delivery. I was told that some women are provided with looped ropes tied to the rafters for them to hold onto in case the delivery is difficult; however, I did not see this while in the barrio. Pushing hard against the foot brace and holding steadfast to the rope, according to informants, eases the labor pain. The husband normally stays kneeling behind the wife, holding her by the shoulders to comfort and give her the necessary encouragement in her labor.

At the moment of birth the midwife presses strongly with both hands at the point just above the mother's belly to push the baby out and to prevent blood from flowing up to her head. If this is not done, the baby would return to its original position in the womb as soon as its head hit against the opening of the birth canal and the mother would become unconscious should blood flow up to her head. Birth will then be delayed and the woman will suffer hemorrhage and may die. Thus all the necessary precautions are taken during delivery.

Some precautions have touches of the supernatural. For example, windows and other openings are closed and covered with old clothes in order to prevent "bad air" and evil spirits from coming in. Blood coming out of a woman during birth is said to smell sweet "like ripe jackfruit" and this attracts the environmental spirits. It is fortunate if the good spirits arrive first because they can shield the mother and the child with protective charms, but if the evil ones arrive ahead, both the mother and her baby are endangered.

As soon as a baby is born and out of danger, the midwife puts it aside and attends to the mother. She tightens a *bigkis* or binder around the upper portion of the mother's belly to prevent hemorrhage. Supporting the lower portion of the belly with her hands, she at the same time applies gradual pressure to expel the placenta. As soon as the placenta is out, another binder is tied around the belly to prevent the expansion of the uterus during puerperium.

With the mother out of danger, the midwife turns to the baby once more. She takes its umbilical cord and stretches this up to its forehead and, tying it at this point with a piece of thread, she cuts the extra cord off with a bamboo splint. The remaining cord is tied at the base with another piece of thread. The infant's lips and cheeks are smeared with blood from the wound so that these will become rosy, a desirable sign of good health. Fresh ashes from the "eye of the hearth" are applied to the remaining end of the cord, which is then rolled and wrapped with a piece of clean cloth sewed to form a bag. Scrappings from coconut shells and another pick of clean ashes are applied around the base of the cord—the portion close to the abdomen of the infant. It is believed that the scrappings and the ashes hasten up the curing and removal of the cord.

The midwife gives the newborn a sponge bath of lukewarm water after everything has been carefully taken care of. Oil is rubbed all over the baby's body before dressing it. Then a banana inflorescence, known as *puso?*, is secured and placed beside the child. This is done to influence blood to flow freely through the baby's veins. Prepared juice from pounded leaves of a plant called *?amargoso* is next given to the child to cause it to vomit "the old blood it derived from the mother." According to a midwife, if it does not eject this old blood, the child will never grow stout and will be thin and sickly throughout life. The newborn is bathed three days later.

Post-delivery treatment   After the placenta has been expelled the midwife secures leaves of medicinal plants which she makes into a *pangalap* or charms against evil spirits. When I asked for the names of the plants, the midwife refused to tell, saying that "the plants will lose their healing powers should I do so." At any rate, part of these leaves is wilted, wrapped with thin cloth, and applied, while hot, on the uterus to hasten the healing of lesions. The other part is poulticed around the belly to prevent swelling of the abdomen. She is next given a bowl of a bitter-tasting concoction (*kuyum*) made of soot and ginger "in order to prevent inflammation of the womb."

For nine days the mother and child are kept from being exposed to the open air. Windows are kept closed and the recuperating mother is not allowed to do any work except to attend to her baby. The lights are not put out at night and should the baby fret and cry, the men of the house stay awake. The belief current in Malitbog is to the effect that immediately after birth a supernatural being named *Patangdo?* comes around to determine the baby's life-span and the manner of its death. Its fretting and crying means that it is talking to *Patangdo?*.

During the nine-day post-delivery confinement, the midwife comes daily to massage the mother. On the ninth day, she is bathed with lukewarm water mixed with a decoction of beeswax and the leaves of several medicinal plants. While at bath, the room is enclosed with blankets to keep out "evil spirits." The hair of the mother, however, is washed with cold water and dried immediately. Coconut oil is rubbed all over the body and the hair is smoothen with it. Then she is made to sit on a chair especially made for the purpose. This is covered with another blanket and the "roasting" begins, a process designed to hasten the healing of the uterus. The boiled leaves for the bath form part of the "smoking" paraphernalia. Smoking lasts until the woman perspires profusely, when the blanket is removed and her perspiration is wiped. The woman is made to lie down again and another massage session is held. This is called *sola,* a ritual massage intended to strengthen the mother's body against the environmental spirits.

Convalescence is known as *panghinguli?* (to return to the former physical state). The mother strictly observes food taboos during the period to insure her steady flow of milk. The two categories of food in Malitbog are the "cold" and the "hot" foods. Hot foods are bad for the nursing mother. These include jackfruits, breadfruits, mangoes, and starchy tubers of plants known as *gabi.* Pork and fatty foods are avoided because these stop lactation. Gelatinuous rice, cooked cornmeal, and sweet potatoes are also avoided; otherwise, the convalescing mother will suffer *boghat* (relapse). Vegetables, white rice, and seafood are considered cold foods and are good for the nursing mother; chickens and eggs are also prescribed as good for lactation.

4 / From infancy to weaning

THE BIRTH OF A CHILD does not disrupt the normal activities of a Malitbog household, except those of the mother. She is not allowed to do hard work until her first bath, which she takes on the ninth day after delivery. There are also a number of things which she must not do. For example, she is warned not to take food which will affect her lactation; she is to refrain from squatting so as not to suffer hernia; and she is to avoid long exposure to the hearth, much less blow the embers into flame, so as not to develop an enlargement of the throat. She should likewise take extra care not to tire herself or she will suffer from a relapse known as *boghat*.

In the time that the wife is considered too weak to work, the husband takes over the management of the home, if there is no female kin living with them. Of course this seldom happens because there are always close relatives who come and temporarily live with the couple until the wife is strong enough to resume her work. At any rate, when Maxim's wife, Teling, gave birth to their second baby, none of their relatives came. Both husband and wife were immigrants to the place. Choleng and Pedong, the couple's ritual kin, were the only persons who visited them every now and then. However, they did not help in the household work. Maxim washed the *lampin* (diapers) of the child, fetched water, gathered fuel, cooked the meals, bathed the other child, and did many other domestic chores aside from his major agricultural tasks. In spite of this difficulty, Maxim managed to run the house efficiently. He also achieved a status before the eyes of the neighbors; many old folks admired him for his industriousness and used him as an example of a man young girls in the barrio should marry.

In most cases, the burden of taking over the household responsibilities during this period falls on the shoulders of either mother of the spouses. This again depends on whose family of orientation the couple lives at the time of the birth of the child. If they have their own house, the woman's mother is normally sent for; she stays with the couple until the mother's convalescence is over. One reason for this is that "it is the woman's life which is in danger." Moreover, the man's mother may not get along with the daughter-in-law and "she might not attend to her better than the woman's own mother would."

INFANCY

The newly born infant is known as *lapsag* (newcomer). It is considered to be very fragile and soft. Hence it must be carefully handled and protected from noise, from exposure to draft, and, above all, from supernatural spirits. To anticipate all these from happening the mother and child are set off from the rest of the family either by an *ʔamakan* (bamboo mat) wall or by an improvised partition made of blankets and old clothes. Visitors are allowed to see the infant and the mother only after the midwife has performed the necessary rituals. Old folk around always remind those who pass by to say *Purya ʔusug lang* [May my *ʔusug* (breath) not harm you] before touching or peering over the newborn. The people in Malitbog believe that everyone possesses an illness-inducing breath. This comes from inside of the body (some say from the liver, others say from the stomach) and comes out through the pulse, the eyes, and the mouth (by the first word spoken). Should the pulse of two individuals beat at the same time their eyes meet, the one who utters the first word casts an *ʔusug* power over the other. The *ʔusug* causes severe stomach ache. It can be cured only by applying the saliva of the person with the stronger *ʔusug* power on the stomach of the victim.

> Bilin went home one afternoon after a short visit at the neighbor's house. She hardly reached home when the neighbor's son came running after her. When asked what he wanted, the boy said he was sent by his mother to call for Bilin because his younger sister (a seven-month-old baby) was crying hard after she left.
> At first Bilin refused to return: "Why—am I a witch? Or a sorcerer? I have nothing to do with the crying of the child." However, the boy insisted saying that "you might have cast an *ʔusug* on my little sister." Bilin's mother also prevailed upon her to help the child. "Pity the child," the mother said. So Bilin went back.
> The baby was crying hard when they arrived. Bilin drenched her index and middle fingers with saliva and applied these on the stomach of the infant. Momentarily the baby stopped crying and went to sleep.

Because infants cannot talk, they are liable to die from *ʔusug;* hence all known protective measures are followed. Windows are closed and big slits on the floor are covered. The *ʔusug* power is not the sole possession of humans; supernatural beings also have *ʔusug*. In case these nonhumans enter into the house, through the slits or windows, they can cast *ʔusug* both on the mother and the child. It is said that medical doctors cannot cure the *ʔusug*. The illness is outside the province of medical science; it belongs to the realm of the supernatural.

Aside from the *ʔusug* there is another illness-inducing force inherent in spoken words and human breath. This is the *ʔabay*. There is no corresponding English term for this local concept, but it is very close to "inner or psychic predisposition to illness or ill luck." The old folk always warn those who greet the newborn for the first time by saying: *"ʔabayan lang"* ("May you grow without any predisposition to ill luck." or "May my *ʔabay* not befall on you so you will remain healthy."). A sign that the child has been *na ʔabayan* is a sudden change in his physical condition. If he is born healthy, he will become thin and sickly. People say that, like the *ʔusug, ʔabay* cannot be cured by medical doctors; only the local healer can do so. "Take the case of Incio," Ador, a father of five, said when some young informants mumbled doubts about the ?*abay.* "Did the doctors cure his son? Bha—someone tell me."

> Incio had a two-month-old son who suddenly lost his appetite and within a week became very sickly and thin. Incio's wife, a relative of the town nurse, brought the baby to the medical center. The illness was diagnosed as caused by intestinal parasites. The doctors gave the baby medicine.
>
> However, the baby remained sickly and, after two months, it was apparent that he would not recover. Incio called for Elda, the midwife, to treat the baby in spite of the objections of his wife. After the usual ritual diagnoses, Elda said that the baby was *na* ?*abayan.* So she asked the mother who was the last person to greet the child. The mother named the person, and Elda went to him. The man remembered having commented on the health of the infant and willingly complied with Elda's request to treat the baby. The man drenched the baby's navel with saliva and Elda applied ginger on the pulse, forehead, and sole of the feet.
>
> The baby recovered and became healthy thereafter!

If within three days after birth the infant frets and cries, the father builds a bonfire underneath the house. Fretting is interpreted, as I have already indicated, as a sign that the infant is being visited by the evil spirits. Children are believed to be sensitive to the presence of these nonhumans; in fact, they can talk to them. The mother and the child are made to sit directly above the bonfire. The flame is put out to allow the smoke to rise, thus fumigating the two. This is known as *tu?ub.* The smoke "shields the doors, the windows, and the crevices with preventive powers." Sometimes, the uncleaned, topmost part of the *bagakay* reed are placed at the corners of the ground space underneath the house for a similar purpose. If the baby continues to fret, however, the *baylan* (medium) is called and, together with the father, slashes with a bolo the air or suspicious parts of the house to drive away the *maligno* (evil spirits).

The mother is the only person, other than the midwife, who has direct access to the infant during the first two weeks. The father and the grandmother may tend to the baby, but they have to perform a ritual first, like washing their hands and faces, changing their clothes, and fumigating their palms before holding the newborn. This is done because the first two weeks are considered the most dangerous period in the baby's life. He is not yet physically strong and is susceptible to rashes, diarrhea, parasites, and other ailments.

Carefully wrapped with thick *lampin,* the infant is laid beside the mother. He remains in this position most of the time, except when the mother has to move his head from one side to the other in order to prevent acquiring a cranial deformity known as *lipid.* The *lampin* is changed as frequently as the infant wets. *Lampin* wet with urine are not washed immediately; the mother or the midwife simply wrings them well and hangs them to dry. They are again ready for use as soon as dry because urine is not considered "dirty" in that it comes from babies that have not yet drunk water or any beverage. However, if the *lampin* are soiled with feces, these are immediately washed, because "reusing them without removing the feces will make the baby sick." Feces are considered dirt in that they attract flies.

INFANT-FEEDING PRACTICES

As already indicated, the child is not breast fed immediately after delivery, because the colostrum is considered bad for the neonate. Breast feeding takes place on the third or fourth day, depending upon the mother's lactation. If her milk does not come on the third day, the mother takes seafood, beef, stewed chicken, thin porridge with cocoa and sugar, green leaves of sweet potatoes, and other milk-inducing foods. She is enjoined to take plenty of water and broth. If partaking of these food brings no immediate positive results, some rituals are performed. The mother secures a clean half-coconut shell into which she places boiled water. She allows the water to cool overnight, and the following morning she dips her nipples into it. This is believed effective in hastening the coming of milk. Some mothers comb their breast downward every morning with combs made of turtle shells. Others request the midwife to massage their backs. Usually milk comes on the third day. Meanwhile the baby is breast fed by a neighbor who is nursing at the time. If there is no such neighbor, canned milk is purchased in town and given as a substitute. Some mothers feed their two-day-old babies lukewarm rice water.

There are no ceremonies connected with breast feeding in Malitbog. The baby is simply made to feel the mother's breast with its lips, an activity known as *patakmoꞋ*. Thereafter, he is given the nipples if he cries. I have not seen mothers wash their breasts before feeding. Feeding is done by suckling the infant in a prone position, the mother lying on her side, until about a week after having given birth, at which time the mother is strong enough to sit. When feeding in a sitting position, the mother either cuddles the child in her arms and holds him close to the breasts, or let him lie across her folded thighs and she bends a little to feed him.

After feeding, the baby is not lifted from his *lampin* and made to burp because "he might break his neck." The people believe that within two weeks after birth the baby's neck "is not yet strong to carry his head." He is too fragile to be moved about often. Moreover, many people consider it bad "to make the child look over the mother's shoulders during this time; it will shorten his life."

STAGES OF GROWTH AMONG INFANTS

There are different phases of child development known to the people of Malitbog. Each phase is distinguished from the others by responses the child makes to his environment, changes in his physical constitution, the role he plays in group life, and his age in terms of months. Local practices and beliefs also vary according to these stages of development. The people are aware that there are kinds of behavior that are appropriate for each phase as well as responsibilities and privileges that go along with maturity.

A month-old child is known as *harapitən ka hangin*. Literally, the term means "can be carried away by the wind." This is based on responses the child makes each time a waft of soft breeze passes over his face—that is, he smiles and stretches his limbs. Sleep is continuous, except when he is hungry and wet. There is no time schedule for feeding; the breast is given each time he cries. If the mother attempts to maintain a schedule, the other members of the family, especially the older folks, will be angry. Crying is associated with hunger, and the mother is scolded if she does not immediately attend to the baby's needs. Thus when Tio C. came home from the field and heard his grandson's unheeded cries, he shouted at the top of his voice: *"Linti?* [lightning]—would somebody pick up the baby? You want him to die crying?" Husing, the daughter and mother of the child, came running from the kitchen and took the baby in her arms.

The baby is, by this time, the center of adult attention. When he cries or frets, he is picked up, cuddled, and carried around the house, gently pacified with a song or a chuckling sound. Sometimes the baby is rocked in the hammock, a popular piece of household furniture in Malitbog. No house is apparently complete without it. Whether cuddled in the arms or placed in the hammock, the baby is often kissed and talked to by adults, either naturally or in baby talk.

Although the child is the center of group concern, the amount and quality of attention he receives from other members of the household depends on a number of factors. Among these is the order of birth. The firstborn normally receives the most attention from the parents or grandparents because, as one informant said, "Parents are excited over the first sample of what they are; grandparents are joyed over the arrival of the first grandchild." It is said that the oldest is the most favored and spoiled child. Thus even if he were married, with three children, Loreto was still the favorite son of Tio C. and Tia P. Whenever these two old folks come home with foodstuffs—meat, bread, canned food, fish, and so forth—they send for Loreto, either to eat with them or to bring food to his children. The other siblings have accepted this relationship silently.

The coming of other children evokes a less emotional response from the parents than that of the first child. This does not mean that other children are not welcomed or loved; it simply means that, after the first birth, the mother has acquired an experience in childbirth and therefore is less worried with the next. The father likewise has learned his lessons during the trying moments of delivery. In other words, there is less painful anxiety and waiting for the succeeding births than during the inexperienced days of the first birth. As one mother said: "You get used to having babies after the first born and the experience becomes commonplace."

The place of residence and the economic conditions of parents during the succeeding births also contribute to the manner in which children are cared for. As required by tradition, the newlyweds live with the family of orientation of either spouse for a year or until the birth of the first child. Because they are supported by their parents, the new couple is not so concerned about economic problems. They have more time with the baby. Moreover, the grandparents are there to take care of it when either of them are busy. After they establish their own home, however, the new parents assume new responsibilities and play new roles. They have to work harder than they did before in order to provide economic security for the family. Hence, they have less time for the succeeding babies, which are cared for by the older siblings. When I called Doming and his wife's attention to their apparent neglect of their second daughter, who is covered with rashes and skin infections, they smiled: "Of course, we would like to closely watch over her, but we cannot even take a good breath from our work; we have to earn a living, you know." This comment reflects the attitude of practically all parents in Malitbog.

The other child which receives attention—almost equal to that received by the firstborn—is the *kinagut* (youngest). Because the other children are grown up, the latecomer is considered "the joy of the family." He is the object of concern by almost everybody in the family. The parents can spend more time with him in that their own duties are by this time partly relegated to the older children. A son may watch the carabaos, and this frees the father from some work in the field; an older daughter can do the washing instead of the mother. Of course the parents do the difficult tasks. By this time, too, either or both sets of grandparents come to live with the family. In this way, the youngest "is spoiled by all because he is the last baby in the house."

From two to three months of age the infant is known as *nagabukay* ("he starts to chuckle"). The grown children are allowed to play with him, to carry him around, and to watch over him when asleep. The thick, protective *lampin* is gradually removed and by the third month, the infant is dressed in thin clothing. Except when he is asleep, the child is always carried around, cuddled in the arms of the siblings, the mother, or any other adult member of the family. When restless, he is gently tapped on the buttocks or danced and shaken as the mother sings. Sometimes a member of the family will rock him in the hammock. In all events, the infant is overindulged by everyone in the family.

Because the umbilical cord is by now removed, the mother attends closely to the healing navel. She inspects it every morning. Friends who pass by inquire *"Ano na ʔipuʔ dən pusud na kadya?* [Has its umbilical cord already been removed?]" Even if the umbilical cord is gone, the baby continues to wear his binder. To expel gases in the stomach, known as *ganduk ka busung,* spittle from chewed lime, betel leaves, areca nut, and tobacco is applied.

The five-month-old child is known as *naga ʔukuʔ,* a term derived from the root word *ʔukuʔ* (to coo). The child makes noise with his mouth when cooed at by an adult. Everytime the father comes home from work he goes to the hammock and coos at the baby. "This is the time when the baby makes a fool of his parents," Aming, himself a father of five, said. "However, his smiles and laughter remove fatigue from your aching arms." Almost all adult members of the family take turns in talking to the baby and in playing with him. The baby is tickled, pinched, and kissed. The response he makes evokes amusement from the adults.

When the baby attempts to lie prone on his stomach, toward the end of the fifth month, he is known as *nagatikləb,* a term derived from *kələb* (to turn upside down). Because he is now considered to be strong, he is left to roll about on the floor much longer than before. He is fondled roughly too, held in the arms, and bounced on the mother's lap. From this period to late childhood, parents show great concern over the way a child sleeps. Many Malitbog parents believe that if a child sleeps on his stomach, such a position indicates a future life fraught with difficulties. Others say that the baby will have a shorter adult life. To offset the onset of these troubles the child is made to lie on his back or side. Putting his hand across his forehead is likewise considered to be bad for the infant—sorrows are stored in the child's forehead for his adult life. The mother carefully watches that the child does not assume any of these positions. Gnashing the teeth, an act known as *bagrət,* while asleep is another indication of unlucky life in adulthood. Thus should a child gnash his teeth while asleep, the mother will gently slap his face. The most favorable position for sleep is one with the hands folded across the breast. This means that the child will grow up obedient and religious.

During this period if the child urinates, the adults do not show much concern. In fact, it is the source of delight for friends or relatives. If he urinates while being carried in the arms of a kin or a friend, he will be close to the person. Thus, it is common to witness mothers or any adult prod the baby to urinate on a favorite relative or close friend. Everytime I took hold of a baby in Malitbog, mothers would always smile and say: "Come on baby, urinate on Mr. Ukano." True enough my shirt was sometimes wet with urine. The child, by this time, is also carried around without diapers. Sometimes a folded *lampin,* cut from an old but clean dress, is wrapped around his buttocks to catch the feces in case he defecates. However, it is not used in all cases.

The *tikləb* is followed by the *dalhag* (to slide), the period during which the child sort of "slides" over the bamboo floor. This takes place from five to six months after birth. The floor is cleared of objects which the baby may put into his mouth. He can now be carried around the neighborhood, although before this is done, a ritual is first performed. The mother takes a piece of earth and burns it. The burnt earth is next soaked in water and the infusion is given to the child to drink. On the first day the baby is brought downstairs, the mother again secures a piece of wet clay and crosses the sole of the child's feet with it. This makes him invulnerable against sickness caused by the *ʔusbong ka lupaʔ* (vapor of the earth). It is locally believed that the earth emits an illness-inducing heat which newborns cannot physically resist.

A seven-month-old child is known as *nagapungkuʔ* because he now starts to sit alone. He is considered physically strong enough to be handled more roughly. It is quite common to see adults play with the child during rest hours by putting him down to sit by himself. As the child balances his body to maintain this position, they find it entertaining. A quick hand, however, is always around to prevent the child from falling on the hard floor.

When the child starts to crawl, in the eighth or ninth month, he is known as *nagakamang.* He is now watched closely by the siblings or by any adult member of the family. His movement around the house, however, is not controlled. If he slips and bumps his head against the floor, he is not immediately picked up, unless he cries. Even if he is picked up, he is put back on the floor as soon as he stops crying. He is encouraged to crawl about the living room or the kitchen. *Nagapungkuʔ* is followed by the *panglubaybay,* which takes place in the tenth month. *Panglubaybay* is derived from *lubaybay,* which means "to walk with props." The child starts to walk by holding onto objects like chairs, beds, benches, and so forth. The people of Malitbog do not have prams or perambulators such as are found among the city dwellers.

As soon as the child is capable of standing alone, he has reached the stage known as *bugal.* This also takes place in the tenth month. The parents will often prod him to *bugal* (that is, to stand alone) whenever there are visitors. As soon as the child is able to take steps without the help of props, he is known as *nagatikang·tikang.*

This takes place during the middle of the eleventh to the twelfth month, and continues until about the thirteenth month, when the child walks unaided. On the fourteenth month the child's muscular coordination and balance are quite stable; he walks and runs about the house or in the yard. He is now known as *nagapanaw*. The following tabulation is the summary of the chronology of development of an average Malitbog child:

Local Term	*Approximate Age*	*Associated Activities*
Bagʔong lapsag	Immediately after birth	Sleeps all the time
Harapitən ka hangin	One to two months	Begins to open eyes and to smile
Bukay	Third month	Chuckles and moves arms and legs
ʔukuʔ	Fourth month	Responds to coos
Tikləb	Fifth to sixth months	Attempts to lie on stomach
Dalhag	Sixth to seventh months	Slides on stomach
Pungkuʔ	Eighth month	Attempts to sit alone; coordination begins
Panglubaybay	Ninth month	Stands by holding onto objects
Bugal	Ninth to tenth months	Attempts to stand alone
Tindəg	Tenth to early eleventh months	Stands alone
Tinkang·tikang	End of eleventh to twelfth months	Attempts to walk
Panaw	Thirteenth to fourteenth months onward	Child walks alone, unaided

Breast feeding becomes irregular as soon as a baby starts to teethe because, as most mothers say, "It bites the nipples." Malitbog mothers do not use pacifiers; instead the child is given a corncob, green guava fruits, or other hard objects which are too big to be swallowed. It is not uncommon to see a child lying on the floor playing and biting an object given by the mother or by anyone taking care of him. When the child bites the mother, he receives a hard slap on the buttocks, accompanied by an angry reprimand. Sometimes the feeding is stopped. This frustrates the child and he bounces on the floor, tears his hair, and cries at the top of his voice. Ripe bananas, candies, cooked sweet potatoes, and other foods are given as placebos. Sometimes the mother resumes the breast feeding, but with a warning: "Do not bite my nipples or I will not feed you anymore."

FEEDING PRACTICES IN LATER MONTHS

In feeding the child, the mother, who has now resumed her normal domestic chores, takes care that she does not nurse the young one immediately after she had done strenuous work in the field or after she had exposed herself long under the heat of the sun. She should take a rest or, as one informant puts it, "cool herself first." It is believed that strenuous work and exposure to heat either of the sun or of the kitchen fire makes her milk rancid. If fed with it, the child will have a stomach-ache and loose bowel movements. If the child insists on suckling, the mother cools her nipples in a cup of water. Sometimes she forces the "hot" milk out by pressing her nipples. To be sure that the child does not get sick in case not all of the undesirable milk is removed, the mother smears his navel with the first few drops of the "hot" milk.

Unlike the first few weeks after birth, feeding during this period is done with the least concern on the part of the mother. I have watched mothers nurse their babies while chopping vegetables or playing cards. Feeding is frequently interrupted. The mother may stand up, brush the baby aside, go to the fireside, and return. The baby seems to adjust to the routine, waiting until the mother returns, when he resumes suckling.

Supplementary feeding is introduced as early as the fifth month, when the child is able to turn over by itself. This is necessary if the mother is ill, if she does not have enough milk, or if she cannot devote all her time to the baby owing to a tight work schedule in the field, especially during planting and harvest. The baby's "biting habits" during teething are taken as an indication that he is ready for adult foods.

As the first food other than mother's milk, an occasional spoonful of lukewarm rice water or of thin porridge is given. Later, ripe bananas and mashed boiled sweet potatoes are added. The mother sometimes chews cooked hard food and feeds it to her child. This is called ʔupaʔ and the act of feeding, ʔupaʔ an. It is believed that feeding the child in this manner will make him closer and more loyal to the parents. Whenever anyone comes home with food, the baby's lips are smeared with it. This is to prevent sickness caused by *sabit* (close English translation: "being hurt for not having been given the food").

Increased bowel elimination on the part of the baby resulting from its taking supplementary hard food, starting on the sixth month, is a cause for concern from adult members of the family, especially the father. The mother, however, continues to be tolerant about it. If the child defecates on the floor, the father raises his voice and scolds the one taking care of him. Toilet training starts from the seventh month onward. In defecating the child is lifted by the mother, who makes an opening in the floor, places the baby on his feet, and lets him complete his defecation with such proddings as "ʔuuuuuuuh ʔuuuuuuuh ʔuuuuuuuh." Later, when about a year old, the child is brought to the kitchen, where he defecates through a slit in the bamboo floor near the stove.

Owing to uncleanliness resulting from crawling and moving about the house, children develop skin infections, boils, and rashes, as well as infections of the anal zone, the genitals, and the eyes, causing restlessness and crying, especially at night. Colds, accompanied by coughing and a running nose, are another general cause of irritation and annoyance in children. This is not treated, however, because "all children will have it—it is natural for them to cough or to have running nose." Hiccups, known as *siduʔ*, are conceived to be a sign of growing up. Mothers and other adult members of the family usually comment: "Ha—the child is really growing up rapidly. Listen how he hiccups." Thus, there is no attempt to cure them, unless they become extremely annoying, in which case the mother will give the child some water to drink.

WEANING

The time for weaning a child in Malitbog varies. Some mothers say that a child is weaned after nine months; others say after a year. However, 12 of the 20 mothers in the barrio at the time I carried out this research had not weaned their children, although they ranged in age from one to two years.

The uncertainty of the weaning period was expressed by Ramona, one of the nursing mothers: "I like to wean my baby right away but when he cries, especially at night, I cannot stand it. I pity him. So I decided to let him have his way. Do not laugh because when you will have children of your own, then you will understand." While we were talking, the son came out of the kitchen. He approached the mother and reached for her breasts. Opening her blouse, she put one of her nipples out for the child to suck. The boy suckled eagerly. Noting me watching them, she poked the boy's buttocks gently and said, "Ha—you should be ashamed of yourself—see, Mr. Ukano is watching you. You are too big to suckle, you know."

A child is weaned early should the mother become pregnant before it is one-year old; otherwise, the child will become sickly. Many Malitbog mothers believe that the milk of a pregnant woman is rancid; it is known as *gurang nga gatas,* meaning "mature milk." The fresh milk is for the coming child of the pregnant mother. Therefore, it is bad for the preceding child to take it. A child is also weaned early when the mother becomes ill or when her work schedule in the fields becomes tight during planting and harvesting seasons.

As a transition from infancy to childhood, weaning is often fraught with traumatic experiences. By being deprived of nurture and the comfort of its mother's arms, the child suffers insecurity and emotional stress. That is why many mothers say, "Weaning is sometimes difficult." The period is characterized by crying, temper tantrums, and annoying fussiness. The following display of emotion of a nine-month-old weanling is typical among newly weaned children in Malitbog.

> Jumari was sitting on his mother's lap as she cut green beans for lunch. After finishing, she stood up to wash the pot in the kitchen. Jumari refused to be put down. Nevertheless, his mother brushed him aside and proceeded to the kitchen. The boy started to cry. None of the adults came to his aid. The mother called out from the kitchen: "Oh stop it. I will be with you in a moment."
>
> However, Jumari continued crying, and this time he raised his voice so that he was almost bawling, but the mother did not come. Perspiration appeared on his forehead and mucus oozed out of his nose. He brushed these aside with the back of his little hand and continued crying. When no one still came to him, he rolled over on the floor, kicked, and tore his hair and clothes. An older sibling came, but he refused to be lifted by her.
>
> A neighbor came up to inquire why Jumari was crying. Hearing an unfamiliar voice, the boy stopped crying for a while and then resumed crying, rolling, kicking, and tearing his clothes. Still no one came to pick him up. Finally, he bumped his head against the door until it bled. Thereupon, the adult members of the family, including the mother, came running to him. His older sibling held him, as the mother bandaged the wound. He stopped crying, but continued to gulp sobs and tears rolled down his cheeks. The mother went out to the kitchen and returned with a ripe banana. She took the boy and danced around. Jumari reached for her breast. She suckled the child until he was fast asleep.

Children crying after their mothers; to be left behind is indeed a traumatic experience for these two weanlings.

In spite of this uncontrolled display of emotion, known as *pasinggit,* the child is seldom punished. Parents agree that it is natural for the child to cry and be fussy when he is being weaned. In one instance a father did beat his little girl with a stick when she cried during mealtime and kicked a trayful of rice, but she was punished not because she was fussy or crying, but because she "did not show respect for the food on the table."

To wean a child most mothers rub bitter-tasting juice or elements like ginger, pepper, and soot on their nipples. Others put the excreta of earthworms on the nipples to make them appear dirty. Then the mother will show them to the child: "See —huh—dirty. Don't suckle anymore, the nipples are dirty." One mother applied mercurochrome and told the child that her nipples were hurt and bleeding, therefore he could not have them.

A child is also weaned by frightening him, especially at night when the child cries and begs for the mother's breast: *"Hala—*the *ʔaswang* will come and get you if you do not stop crying." The father or any adult member of the family will come to the mother's aid by making a hissing sound with the lips: "Hissspspppsssspppppsssppp." The mother, in turn, calls the child's attention to it: "Did you hear that? Oh I'm afraid. Come now—stop crying. Certainly the *ʔaswang* will know where you are if you do not stop crying. He must be around, you know. Listen."

A most effective way of weaning a child is, as most mothers attested, "to leave him with the grandmother, the aunts, or a close kin for about two to four months." His separation from the mother makes the child forget the "nipples." If this is not possible, the child's care is assigned to his siblings. He sleeps with them at night. In this way the traumatic effect of abrupt physical separation of the child from the mother is avoided and weaning is facilitated.

Once weaning is accomplished, the mother is relieved of the whining and crying of the baby, but the swelling of her breasts is another source of annoyance. To hasten the "drying of the breast" most Malitbog mothers poultice their breasts with the flowers of the male papaya. Others drink a concoction prepared by a midwife.

5 / Childhood and formal education

C HILDHOOD BEGINS as soon as a child is weaned. As a child, the treatment he receives from the adults begins to change. The tolerance he enjoyed during infancy, for example, is gradually withdrawn, and pressures are brought to bear upon him to follow adult standards of proper behavior. In defecating he is told to use the slit in the floor behind the stove or the *kasilyas* (a privy constructed close to the back part of the house); he can no longer urinate anywhere he likes. He is free to move about the house and in the yard, but he is punished should he do the improper thing; he is shouted at and scolded when he carelessly stumbles and cries. He is disturbed even when sleeping and resting. Adults no longer give him support and protection against the frightening darkness of the night when the sounds of insects and animals are loud and seem dangerous. His cries for security during these moments are deemed unreasonable; his requests for food to assuage the gnawing pain of hunger at night, annoying. Suddenly, the world becomes indifferent and full of contradictions. He is not allowed to understand this world, but he is forced to conform to its demand.

In this chapter, I shall discuss how this world is formed in the mind of the child by describing the various steps he undergoes in learning the basic values of adult society.

PALAWAS (EARLY CHILDHOOD)

As soon as the child begins to walk and to subsist on hard food he enters into another phase of development known as *palawas*, meaning "to grow nodes, as in a bamboo." In terms of local concepts of human growth, this means "to gain height by becoming thin." Thinning is a prerequisite to human development as acquiring nodes is to a growing reed, runs a popular Malitbog proverb. This covers the period between one-and-a-half and seven years of age. The child is by now expected to adjust to adult demands which are completely contrary to those made during infanthood. Even his feeding habits must be adjusted to the work schedules of the adults, and because of poor diet, normally consisting of rice and dried fish, he becomes susceptible to various ailments. Because these are seen, however, as part of growing up, the child does not receive medical attention for them. Of the 104 children, ranging in age from six to ten, whom I closely observed from 1964 to 1965, 75 were confined in bed for various illness during different times of the year; the rest suffered from mild influenza.

The mother continues to show concern over the daily activities of the child. She sees to it that he is fed and sleeps comfortably with siblings; he is bathed regularly. The greater part of this task, however, is taken over by the older siblings, who stay with the small child at home most of the time. Parents spend less time with their children after they have been weaned. Siblings, aunts, cousins, and grandparents take part, alternately, in overseeing the activities of the child during the day.

As soon as the child is physically strong enough to move around, he spends most of his time outside of the house—playing in the yard with other children. Apparently, it is in games and other peer-group interactions that the child finds release from the stresses and strains of restrictive disciplines that characterized the months following his weaning. Thus, it is common to see a small child cry and kick in tantrums when his siblings refuse to allow him to play with them or with other children. Once at play, however, he is persuaded to come home only with difficulty, unless he is hungry. Sometimes even his meals are forgotten. I have often watched small children of about the same age become so absorbed in their play—catching dragonflies, digging holes in the ground, measuring sand with bottle covers, gathering tiny stones or piling little sticks—that no one spoke for almost an hour. The siblings assigned to take care of them were also among their own peers, engrossed in their own games—climbing trees, running a race, picking wild fruits, or playing house. Peer-group association, in other words, begins early in Malitbog and continues to be the potent organizing mechanism in the local adult culture.

Play groups consist, mainly, as I have already indicated, of siblings and cousins. Most neighbors in Malitbog are related. Games played vary from day to day, depending upon the preference of the players. If a game is unfinished, it is resumed the following day to settle the problem of who won it. Otherwise, a different game is played.

The *tumbang patis* (the fallen can), which consists of hitting a tin can with a stone called *butanwan,* is the most common game played by both sexes. One acts as an *it* and two or more children take turns in hitting the can with their *butanwan.* The *it* replaces the can every time it is hit, watching the owners to retrieve their *butanwan,* and anyone who is caught becomes the *it.* I have seen children in this game do ingenuous tricks and maneuvers in order to escape being the *it.* Some are really skillful in the game. It is very exhausting and long, often characterized by shouting, running, and quarreling.

"Gun fighting" with bamboo popguns is popular among boys. Adults sometimes participate in this game by acting as umpires. Dividing themselves into groups and mimicking soldiers, children shoot each other. "Bang! bang! Hala—you are dead, you are dead." Certain rules are followed in this game. For instance, the first one to shout "Bang! bang!" wins the game, and the other child feigns being dead. Nonobservance of this rule gives rise to constant quarrels, but most of the time, children observe it strictly. The rule breaker is censured as *madaya?* and no one will play with him again.

The types of games played depend upon the children's age and sex. Small children content themselves with simple games like pulling an empty coconut shell or tin cans of sardines. Spinning tops and flying kites are popular only among boys. Indeed, these are games for boys from which girls are particularly told to keep away. Doll playing is for girls, and boys are likewise expected to refrain from joining; those who insist are teased as being *ʔagiʔ* (effeminate).

Shotbung is a popular outdoor game participated in by both sexes, and is played either during the day or evening, the latter time being the most preferred. This game is similar to *tumbang patis* in that a tin can is used; the difference lies in the procedure. The first *it* is chosen by lot among the players if no one volunteers for the position. The other children hide behind walls, under the house, behind the bushes, and other places. The *it* looks for them, at the same time keeping close watch on the tin can; if it is kicked or thrown away by the players, his period of being *it* will be prolonged. As soon as he spots anyone of the players, he shouts: "Bong" before the player hits the can. The first player to be "Bong" becomes the *it*. Violation of this rule often ends in quarreling, shouting, and fighting among the children.

Most indoor games consist of playing "carabao," hide and seek, dropping handkerchiefs, and *buta·buta* (blindfolding the *it*). These games are played when it is raining, or in the evening when it is dark outside. Indoor games are less boisterous than outdoor ones, because parents are present to oversee the players' activities.

There are many other games which children in Malitbog play. Among these are *bəyəp·bəyəp* (a betting game done by blowing two or more rubber bands out of a circle), *tirung* (a betting game with beans for stakes), *bogʔoy* (another betting game with seashells for stakes), hole-ins, running a race, and so on. Because games are seldom played individually, the child learns early about teamwork, role playing, and discipline. He also gains through these activities an understanding of norms governing group behavior.

This learning process is reinforced by other forms of adult discipline. The most common of these is frightening the crying child with the *ʔaswang:* "Keep silent or the *ʔaswang* will come to take you." Sometimes parents or any member of the family will pretend to hear the noise of the *tiktik* or the *wakwak,* which is an indication of the presence of an evil spirit, or of the *ʔaswang.* Then the mother will ask the child: "What is it? Did you hear that? Now you'd better behave or I will leave you alone."

Old folks are often called to frighten a child: "*Hala*—old man————[mentions the name] is coming to take you. Better come here and be a good child," one would tell the fretting sibling. Preternatural beings known as *sigbin* are also mentioned. A *sigbin* is believed to roam around during the night and harm children; the activities are mentioned in Malitbog mythology. Ghosts and *kapri* (a black, hairy man) are other superntaural beings also mentioned to frighten the child.

Threats of castration is another common form of frightening an unruly child. An old man who sees a crying boy will stop and, in a raised voice, say: "Huh—stop crying or I will cut off your testicles. Do you like to be a *kapun* [castrated]?" Misbehaving girls are threatened with having their clitoris pinched. A mother will say: "Stop misbehaving or I will pull your clitoris out." Or an annoyed grandmother will shout: "Stop your crying and be a good girl or I will pull your clitoris and wind it around your neck."

Slapping with the hands and beating with a piece of stick are forms of punishments. The unheedful child is also pinched. A quote from my field notes substantiates this.

> *February 8, 1964.* Early this morning Tonyo, a newly weaned son of Raming, asked for something to eat and breakfast was not yet ready. His sister gave him a piece of ripe banana, but he refused. He kept on crying for about ten minutes, insisting on cooked sweet potatoes. Pestered by his crying, the mother stepped out of the kitchen and slapped his mouth, saying: *"Magahəd!* Stop making noise or I will beat you some more." However, the boy did not stop. She took a piece of stick and threatened to hit him. The boy stopped.

Eating habits of children are regulated immediately after weaning. Much threatening and beating occur during this period. When a child begins to be choosy about foods, he is punished. I have observed a mother slap and lecture a child for refusing a food being served: *"Hala*—you eat. Don't you dare throw the rice away or I'll skin your buttocks." To be choosy about food is to incur the wrath of the *gabaʔ*, and the child is taught about this early in life.

A child who eats in the house of a neighbor is scolded. Although it is not explicitly stated, if the act becomes habitual it becomes embarrassing to the family because, as one informant said, "People might think parents are not feeding the child." Also, once food is accepted from neighbors—even if they are relatives—it starts a vicious cycle of food exchange locally known as *garalwanay.* As some informants said:

> It is good if you always have good viands. If not, you are merely shaming yourself before your neighbors. Good if they will eat what you send; if they do not like it, they throw it to the pigs or feed it to the dogs. Imagine!

Exchanging food is practiced among neighbors, nonetheless, though in a limited way. For example, if a family had dressed a chicken or had brought home some foodstuffs, meat or fish, a portion of these, or a plateful when cooked, is sent to the immediate neighbor—usually a very close relative. In doing so, one is sure that the food will be received graciously and eaten.

Children are taught not to receive foods from strangers, although this is often unheeded. Parents always warn them that "accepting food from people you do not know is dangerous. What happens if he is an *ʔaswang*—huh—you will surely be bewitched." Local belief tells that one becomes an *ʔaswang* through food and drinks received from strangers. The *ʔaswang* simply drenches the food with his saliva or mixes it with the drinks, like *tuba.* Whoever partakes of the food or drinks the beverage is bewitched, known as *yangaw.*

Accepting food is censured because of fear of social exposure. Accepting food, in terms of local norms, means accepting the fact that the family is economically short of the basic staple. Of course, lack of supply throughout the year is openly discussed, even with strangers, because it is felt that such people might be government officials who might be able to help. However, this must be done discriminately. The prevailing feeling of "shame" accounts for this reticence, and the child has to be taught this norm early.

"Stealing food is very common among children, although food is never hidden from them. To hide food from children is considered bad. As one mother explained:

A group of children eating green seeds from pods of a tree known as ʔaghoʔ (Leucaena glauca [*Linn.*] *Benth*).

Children in their Sunday best.

"Why keep food from children? It is *kagəragtəs* [courting ill luck]. You labor hard to feed the children and why should you keep the food from them?" Sugar balls in the basket and cold rice in the pot are the frequently "stolen" foods. Fruits are also "stolen." Stealing may not be the right word for these early childhood pranks. The term "taking" might be most appropriate because at this age the child is least aware of the moral implications of his actions. Insofar as he is concerned, this is part of the daily activities. At any rate, mothers keep the food from children only when it is reserved for the succeeding meal or for someone who has not yet eaten, with the stern warning: "This is not to be touched."

Children normally eat with their parents, although they are sometimes fed first in order to avoid quarreling, fighting, and crying over choice slices of viands. They are never allowed to eat with visitors. "It is embarrassing when there are visitors and children fight. Of course children are children, but some people might think we do not discipline our young ones," explained one mother. Like adults, children eat with their hands, since the use of spoon and fork is not ordinarily availed of by the family in the first place; silverware is reserved for visitors.

Sharing food with siblings and playmates is taught early among children. Parents enjoin even the one-year-olds to share what they have with their brothers and sisters. Older siblings are constantly reminded not to be selfish. As the mother or caretaker gives the child a banana, boiled sweet potato, bread, or candies, for example, she tells him, "Come now, share it with your brothers and sisters." In spite of this emphasis on the value of sharing, conflicts among children occur when the adult members of the family bring home sweets and goodies like rice cakes and sugar balls. Whoever appropriates such treats first seldom shares them with others until he is satisfied, so other siblings take them by force and intimidation. Crying, tantrums, and fighting occur, usually ending up with all protagonists being slapped or whipped.

The cleanliness of children is often neglected. They go about the yard with unwashed hands and faces. Occasionally adults remind them of their being dirty, but this is about all that is done. No strict rules for cleanliness are followed. There is no one to enforce them anyway, for parents are out most of the time—in the fields or in town earning a living; siblings who are charged with caring for the young ones are also busy playing around the house.

Children over one year old are still bathed by their mothers. The bathing place is a nearby creek. Laundry soap is often used because toilet soap costs more than most can afford. Clothes being worn are seldom changed. When those worn by a child need washing, they are removed, immersed in soapy water, squeezed, wringed dry, and worn again still wet. It is not thought that colds are caught this way. In fact, mothers contend that wearing wet clothes is desirable for children because (a) it cools the body; (b) it cures the *butod* (enlargement of the stomach due to "heat emanating from the body"); and (c) it cools the "hot" food in the stomach, thus preventing loose bowel movements.

No elaborate ritual is observed when the child has his first haircut after his first birthday. The first haircuttings are kept for medicinal use when the child develops a fever or has convulsions. It is believed that after the child has his first haircut, he becomes sickly and his own hair is the best cure. Portions of the cuttings are burned with native incense, and the sick child is fumigated with it. It is said that the smoke from the hair and native incense has strong curative power.

Children from one to seven years old continue to sleep with either the father or the mother. Parents encourage this arrangement because "it is easier to keep watch over them at night." Evil spirits are said to roam around during the night, and if children are not watched, "they might be snatched or harmed while asleep." Because of this belief, even sick children are not separated from their siblings or parents. Thus disease spreads rapidly. Once a member of a family becomes sick, for example, with influenza, all other members will also have the same ailment. That a disease is contagious is seldom understood. The people believe that an ailment will not "leave the house until everyone living in it had his share."

Respect for elders is taught early in Malitbog. Small children are often required to kiss the hands of the mother or the father at vesper time. They are also taught to obey their elders. Aside from the basic techniques of threats and actual punishment, bribery is resorted to make a child toe the line of adult behavioral requirements. For example, all "don'ts" are accompanied by a promise of a reward, generally in terms of food. Sometimes the promise is kept, oftentimes it is not. The effect on the child is that he mistrusts other people's words or actions. It is not unlikely that the passive, uncooperative attitudes of the adults, especially with people who are not members of an immediate family, may have developed in part from this early childhood training.

NAKALUʔAD (LATE CHILDHOOD)

Late childhood is known, characteristically, as *nakaluʔad*. During this phase of growth, which covers the period from seven to twelve years, the child is said to become healthy again because "he had thrown out all the health-inhibiting elements from within the body.

Sex differentiation and participation in many work activities begin as soon as the child is old enough to run errands. The boys help in the fields—watching carabaos, plowing, harrowing, fetching water, and cutting firewood. The girls take care of the younger siblings (although the boys may also do this job), help in the kitchen, and assist the mother in her domestic activities. In the field, they also participate in digging sweet potatoes, watching the rice fields for birds, and bringing food to the laborers during the planting and harvesting season.

Parents begin to be stricter with children during this period. Children between the ages of seven and twelve are physically punished by whipping if they make mistakes or if they start to be "annoying" to the parents. If during mealtime the child does not clean his plate, he is slapped and told to finish his meal. Sometimes he is told that he will not grow "if you cannot consume your *sinamo*ʔ [rice mixed with viands]." If a child comes late into the house during mealtime, he is scolded by any of the older members of the family; repetition is regarded as defiance, and he is therefore punished by whipping. Most parents I interviewed expressed the view that whipping is necessary "and should be done in order to discipline the child." This consensus of opinion finds support in the permission parents have given to the schoolteachers "to use corporal punishment if necessary because whipping is the only disciplinary measure most children recognize."

Respect for parents and all adult kin is constantly emphasized during late-childhood years. Obedience is stressed; answering back when reprimanded and passing in front of people talking without asking permission are not tolerated. A child should keep silent when adults are conversing. Generosity is also reemphasized by requiring a child to share food and playthings with other siblings or kin.

During this period, children show signs of aggression. In fact, sibling rivalry, which normally begins at weaning, becomes more marked—older siblings start to boss the younger ones, to push them around whenever they can, and to make them cry. Parents enter the scene and punish the culprit. Sometimes favoritism comes to the fore. The mother seldom punishes her favorite child, and this generates further conflict among the siblings and between herself and her husband. Good neighbor relationships are at times severed mainly because of such conflicts. Here is a case.

> Renito and Simeon were playing near the creek. The former jokingly pushed the latter into the mudhole. Simeon went home and told his mother about it. Angered, Felisa, the mother, went to the creek and spanked Renito. The boy cried and this was heard by his mother, Nelia. She also went to the creek and confronted Felisa to explain why she was hitting the boy. When informed, she asked her son to explain and Renito informed his mother that it was Simeon who started the game. "I merely retaliated," the boy said.
>
> "So it was your child who started the game. Why don't you beat him too," Nelia said.
>
> "Your son is telling a lie," Felisa shouted, waving her stick at Renito.
>
> Soon the two mothers were shouting at each other. Felisa lunged at Renito with the intention of hitting him again. However, Nelia caught her by the hair and threw her to the ground. When Felisa came to her feet, she attacked Nelia and they dropped to the ground, clawing, scratching, and hitting each other.
>
> The entire neighborhood was agog. Many people soon came to see the fight. The men separated and pacified both protagonists. After this incident the women did not talk to each other for several months.

Industriousness is one trait parents expect of their children. Laziness is censured and is used as the criterion for preferential treatment of children and for distinguishing between children as food consumers and food producers. To produce and to give food means love, affection, protection, obedience, and respect; but unwillingness to work means daily reproaches from parents and adult members of the family. The psychological affect of reproaches on the child's behavior is noticeable. Quite often the child, when ordered to perform a task, simply refuses to obey because having been told so often that he is lazy, he has come to believe it. This continuous pattern of chaffing and reprimanding a child soon makes him indifferent to orders and to parental authority.

FORMAL EDUCATION

The school is one of the local institutions in the barrio which needs to be mentioned because of its significance to child training and, consequently, to adult behavior. As noted earlier, there is a two-room schoolhouse located in the middle of the

A boy carrying a half-filled sack of rice on his head.

A two-room schoolhouse located in the center of Malitbog.

barrio. It is government operated and is locally managed by two female teachers who handle four classes. These teachers, residents of the nearby barrio, hold BSEED (Bachelor of Science in Elementary Education) degrees and are graduates of a local college and a university in Iloilo city. Miss P., the younger teacher, handles grades 1 and 2 and Miss M., the older one, handles grades 3 and 4.

Because of lack of facilities, each room of this two-room schoolhouse accommodates pupils of different grades. Thus first graders are mixed with second graders in room A and so are third graders mixed with fourth graders in room B. Miss P. handles this situation quite efficiently. As the class begins for the day, she tells the pupils to stand and sing songs which both grades know. Then she faces the second graders and gives them writing assignments. Writing is done by copying the alphabet at the blackboard. When the second graders are busy, she faces the first graders and gives them the necessary instructions for the day. The same method is used by Miss M. in her mixed-group classes.

Opening of classes in Malitbog Elementary School follows the national school-year calendar. Age admission is seven and above. For the school year 1964–1965, there were no six-year-old children admitted. There had been some bickering in this regard, however. Children whose seventh birthday fell in months after enrollment day had to wait until the following year in order to be admitted. Some parents protested against this, arguing that "the child will be seven next month." However, the teachers remained adamant. Rules are rules, and the teachers often win.

The medium of instruction in the first grade is the vernacular. The second grade gets the first vocabulary in the national language (Tagalog). This is continued up to the third grade, although here English is added. Both the vernacular and English are used for giving instruction. The effect of this burden in linguistic learning to the mental development of the school child is difficult to assess in that many teachers, including those in Malitbog, say that the child reads rapidly when the medium of instruction is the vernacular. My observation in this respect, however, insofar as the fourth-grade adults in Malitbog are concerned, indicates that none of these languages are mastered as effective means of "literate communication." After a few years outside of the school, those who finished the first four years of elementary education are just as illiterate as those who have not gone to school at all.

The first day in school is a traumatic experience for those who have no siblings already attending classes or for those who come from a far sitio and are entering the place for the first time. One usually hears crying, bawling, cajoling, scolding, and threatening from the child, the parents, siblings, and teachers during the first day in school. This case typifies the yearly scene in the Malitbog schoolhouse:

> Berting, eldest son of Talyo and Anding, was enrolled by the mother one week before classes began. A day before school opened, he was very proud and excited about going to school. He went around the neighborhood telling other non-school-age children that "tomorrow I am going to school. My mother will take me there. She bought me a pair of new short pants, a school bag, paper, and a pencil. See?" He carried the bag around for the other children to admire. Everyone wanted to touch it.
>   The following day, Berting and his mother went to school. Berting, on seeing a crowd of children he did not know, started to show signs of insecurity. He did not dare let go of his mother's skirt. None of his playmates were there. Each face seemed unfamiliar. No cajoling from anyone would make him release his mother.

Finally, the teacher requested the mother to accompany Berting inside the classroom. This made the boy walk to the designated seat. Attracting his attention with a writing pad, the teacher was able to make Berting release his mother's hand. The latter immediately stood and left the room.

When Berting realized this, he gave a loud cry. The teacher held him. However, he clawed and bit. He cried so hard that he frightened the other children. Soon two boys joined him in crying. Berting struggled, but the teacher held him back firmly. When the tug-of-war did not help, Berting kicked the teacher. She let go of his hand. Berting ran toward the door. The teacher grabbed him back, and he shouted and cried again, but he could not get away. So he threw himself to the ground and rolled. This dirtied his clothes.

Outside, the mother fidgeted. She peeped through the window. Berting was able to release himself from the teacher after a while. He ran to the door and into his mother's arms. The mother, quite embarrassed, took him. The teacher told her to take Berting home and to return the following day.

It is not uncommon to see mothers and siblings stay in school for about a week following the opening of classes. Sometimes the teachers request them to do so until the new pupils have become adjusted to the classroom activities and school routines. Often the child will not come to school unless accompanied by a sibling or one of the parents.

Classes begin at 7:45 A.M. and end at about 11:30. Recess is from 8:45 to 9:00 A.M. Much of interaction goes on during recess period when the children are allowed to run around the schoolhouse and are encouraged to play in groups. Sometimes the teacher leads them in a tug-of-war, in running a race, and in many other games. This group play is apparently very effective in building up self-confidence among the children and in facilitating their adjustment to the new environment. Afternoon classes begin at 1:30 and end at 4:30 P.M. with a recess period at 3:30 P.M.

Reinforcing this group interaction is the gradual exploitation, through the help of the mother or other siblings, of kinship relationship. In this strange world outside of the home, the child realizes for the first time that he needs the support and assistance of other children, especially relatives. Thus during the week that mothers and older siblings take the children to school, they often point out to the child who his kin are in the school and why it is important that they should know each other. A bigger kin becomes, automatically, the protector of the younger ones. For example:

Jaime, the ten-year-old son of Amon, was already in the third grade when Berto, his first cousin, was enrolled by the mother in 1964. During the first week in school, Berto had a quarrel with Andres, a "bully" from Sitio Agsiw.

When Jaime found out about this, he accosted Andres after class and asked him, "Why did you destroy the toy of my cousin, Berto?"

"So what?" Andres replied harshly, "he shot me."

"That is not true," Berto said. "I was playing with other boys and he came and took my *pusil pusil* [a popgun made of a small bamboo node]. When I tried to take it back, he broke it."

Two cousins of Andres came to find out what was going on. When Jaime saw this, he called his own cousins. Seeing his kin around, Jaime hit Andres with his fists. They fought. All the kin from both sides acted as referees, but were ready to join a free-for-all should anyone from either side start joining the protagonists.

The teacher came running out of the schoolroom. She separated the boys and told them that if they did not stop fighting they would be reported to their parents. While they were being separated, Andres told Jaime, "Better watch out afterwards."

After the class that afternoon, Jaime, accompanied by his kin, walked home. He gave his books to Berto and he himself carried a long stick. When they reached the creek, located at the foot of the hill, a little distant from the school-house, they found Andres and his kin waiting for them. As before, only Jaime and Andres fought. The other children kept watch.

Older men came along and separated the two boys. Andres suffered a black eye and Jaime a bleeding nose. Their shirts were torn.

After this incident, Andres kept away from Berto. The latter became very close to Jaime, whom he now addressed as "Nong Jaime" [older brother, Jaime].

In addition to kin loyalties, neighborhood consciousness in its wider scope is developed in school. The cohesive element of these early friendship ties become the dominant feature of the Malitbog *kasimaryo* (coming from the same barrio) concept in adult life. In a more or less homogeneous society like Malitbog, neighborhood consciousness and friendship loyalties reinforce the existing kinship ties. Thus even when they are grown up and have their respective families, the people of Malitbog stick to each other in facing problems having to do with the outside world. The barrio becomes the focal point of security and comradeship.

Education in the first grade is simply a matter of memory work. The teacher does all the reciting, explaining to the children the meaning of things in the surrounding world. "Where is the sky?" "Do you see the clouds?" "Where are the boys?" "Who are the girls?" and so on, are among the questions the first-grade child learns in school. All of these questions are asked in the vernacular. The development of self-identity also begins in school. Such questions as: "Who are you?" "What is your name?" "Who is your mother?" "Who is your father?" "Do you have a sister?" "What is your brother's name?" and others, are also asked the child.

Arithmetic learning starts with simple addition. The teacher flashes visual cards with the figures $1 + 1 = 2$, $2 + 2 = 4$, $5 + 5 = 10$, and so forth, written in bold letters. She recites this addition first and later asks the children to repeat it. This is done every day until the children master the material. Addition is followed by subtraction, and then multiplication; later simple division is taught. Solving problems is introduced in the third grade, although in the second grade subtraction with the aid of visual guides like drawings of cats, dogs, and books is used. For example the teacher will ask, "One cat plus one cat equals how many cats?"

Correct answers are praised in public. The teacher smiles and says, "Very good, Julia." She turns to another pupil, "Now Roberto, answer this question. Two dogs plus two dogs equals how many dogs?" Should the child hesitate, he receives proddings from other classmates. Usually the teacher discourages this and punishes the culprit when apprehended.

One morning Miss P. asked Julian to stand up and answer her questions. "There are two carabaos in the field. One went to the river to bathe. How many carabaos are left in the field?" Julian fidgeted for awhile. Other children immediately raised their hands saying: "Mam, mam, mam I, mam I," but the teacher said she was asking Julian. The more the other children insisted on answering the question, the more confused Julian became. Rodrigo, who was seated beside him, pulled his trousers, as a signal to listen; then, he whispered: "One. You say, one." The teacher saw him. She went down the aisle and pulled Rodrigo's ears and made him stand at the back of the classroom, facing the wall. Then she scolded: "Do not teach your classmates. If I see anyone doing it, I will send him out."

The approach to classroom work and problem solving becomes more and more complicated as the child passes from one grade to another. In the fourth grade the child learns geography and the Filipino national heroes, and is expected to be able to read his schoolbooks without help.

Sex differentiation becomes more prominent in school. Girls are asked to sit separately from boys. Even during recess, the boys are told to play with boys, and girls with girls. Outside of the school, however, boys tease the girls or start to play with them, but the teacher is always there to break it up. The sex roles among children become clear-cut. Sweeping the room and yards are duties of girls, while the boys do the cutting and pulling of grass around the schoolhouse. Boys also hoe the garden; girls plant flowers.

Other than this relational training, most of what children learn in school is purely verbal imitation and academic memorization, which do not relate with the activities of the children at home. By the time a child reaches the fourth grade he is expected to be competent in reading, writing, arithmetic, and language study. Except for gardening, no other vocational training is taught. The plants that are required to be cultivated, however, are cabbages, lettuce, okra, and other vegetables which are not normally grown and eaten in the barrio. Seeds of these vegetables are obtained by the teachers from the main school in the *poblacion*.

Sanitation is taught in school, but insofar as my observation went, this is not carried beyond the child's wearing clean clothes. Children may be required to buy toothbrushes, combs, handkerchiefs, and other personal items, and bring these to school for inspection. Because only a few can afford to buy these items, only a few come to school with them. Often these school requirements are the source of troubles at home, a night's crying among the children; parents go to the school and quarrel with the schoolteacher for such "costly requirements which we cannot afford to buy." In the final analysis, such regular school injunctions as "brush your teeth every morning" or "drink milk and eat leafy vegetables" mean nothing to the children. First, none of the families brush their teeth. The toothbrushes the children bring to school are for inspection only. Their parents cannot afford to buy milk. They do not like goats' milk because "it is *malangsa* [foul smelling]."

Cleanliness is conceived by many Malitbog parents as part of the school requirement and not necessarily a habit that a child ought to develop at home. Children who wear their clean clothes at home, for example, are criticized for "acting like a schoolteacher." They are told to wear instead their everyday clothes, usually an old dress, shirt, or short pants. Good clothes are carefully put away so that they can be worn to school the next day. This is a rule which must be strictly followed. I saw children whipped severely for their neglect or for coming home with dirty clothes. One unforgetable incident I had seen involved a nine-year-old boy, Julio. On the way home he played too roughly with other boys and his shirt was ripped badly and his short pants were wet. When his mother, Doray, saw this, she was very mad. She had bought the shirt two days ago. Without much ado, she picked up a piece of stick and whipped the child. Julio writhed in pain and started crying. No one came to his defense; instead, the adults who were present encouraged the mother to "beat him so that next time he will learn to be careful."

The whipping went on for some time. Soon it was apparent that Doray was no longer hitting the boy to discipline him, but to give vent to her anger. Seeing this, Badong, her brother-in-law, came and told Doray to stop. Apparently carried away by her emotion, Doray brushed him aside, saying: "I will teach this child to value my efforts in keeping him dressed." However, Badong held her back. This angered Doray some more. She hit Badong and shouted at him: "Get back. This is my affair and you have no business interfering." The commotion roused the neighborhood. Doray's father came and pacified her. Her sister took Julio to their own house. The boy had bruises all over his body. His eyes were swollen and his voice became hoarse from crying.

Disciplinary methods in school do not differ from those used at home. The school is conceived by parents as a second home of the children, and the teacher is encouraged to deal with a child in much the same way as parents deal with him. In spite of the Department of Education policy against physical punishment, teachers in Malitbog whip and pinch erring children. So far no parents have protested or filed a complaint. I witnessed teachers twisting an erring boy's ears and hitting another with a piece of stick for making faces in the class. When I asked the teacher why she had to do it, her reply was, "That is the only form of discipline they recognize." When I discussed this problem with parents, they were unanimous in saying, "That is the teacher's job. That is good for the children. It will keep them straight." In a word, physical punishment, as a means of disciplining the child, is considered desirable.

Competence in reading by a child is a source of parental delight. Parents often proudly relate how their children can read books, the *Hiligaynon* (a vernacular magazine) and others. Because most Malitbog parents have not gone beyond the sixth grade and many have forgotten their reading and writing skills, the child is not coached at home. All of these skills—reading, writing, and arithmetic—are learned in school. Few parents concern themselves, anyway, with teaching their children; they are too preoccupied with earning a living. Moreover, it is considered the teacher's job to teach the children.

Children are expected to help in the household chores as soon as they arrive from school. If they do not attend to the feeding of the chickens or the pigs, the children are scolded for "thinking only of playing and not of their tasks." Thus, Tia P. shouted at Maria, her granddaughter, for joining the other children in the plaza: "Hoy—you have not yet attended to the pigs. Is playing the only thing your teacher taught you in school? If it is, then, do not go to school anymore; stay here at home and play the whole day. Go—gather vegetables for the pigs. They are hungry."

Chores that children do most frequently after school are gathering fuel, fetching water, and baby-sitting. Baby-sitting is one chore both boys and girls do. If they are playing, however, they merely put the baby aside and allow him to crawl wherever he wants to. If he interferes with the game, he is lifted and put further away. Then the caretaker returns to his play.

Girls are expected to be more modest as soon as they start schooling. They are told how to dress properly. Statements such as "You are now schooling, don't you know that?" are made should the girls misbehave. The boys are likewise reminded that they are now grown up because they are going to school and should therefore behave properly.

Going with the opposite sex begins at home, but it gains prominence in school, particularly during the fourth grade when boys and girls reach the early stage of pubescence. Shyness among girls is considered the proper behavior, and respectfulness is expected among boys. A girl who flirts or who giggles a great deal is censured as *ʔuragən* (sexually hot). Teasing is very popular and it is oftentimes the source of troubles among boys and girls.

6 / Puberty and adolescence

THE PASSAGE FROM CHILDHOOD TO ADOLESCENCE in Malitbog is not marked by special ceremonies, as in many societies. The process is taken in the most casual manner by the adults, and no one talks about it unless asked. Physical changes which occur during these periods are recognized as part of the development of a child into a man or woman. However, these are not considered socially important in determining whether or not an individual is grown up. What is basic, insofar as the people are concerned, is the individual's participation in the social and economic activities of the community. In fact, biological age is an arbitrary criterion for specifying the limits of maturity. A boy of twelve may be considered adult, and is fully accorded that status, if he participates actively in earning a living. On the other hand, a 16-year-old adolescent may still be regarded as a boy if he does not contribute to the family larder. Puberty and adolescence are locally viewed as a configuration of physiological and social phenomena.

In this chapter, puberty and adolescence as concepts of growth are used arbitrarily. The people of Malitbog consider growing up as a part of nature and the terms they use to describe the process are *supang,* the beginning of marked physiological changes, and *hamtung,* the period of advancing maturity. Whether these terms correspond exactly in meaning and in biosocial attributes to puberty and adolescence as understood in the literature is doubted. However, because they are used by the people to characterize the periods of growth between childhood and adulthood, they will be used as approximate points of reference in this study.

SUPANG (PUBERTY)

The Malitbog word which approximates the term "puberty" the most closely is *supang.* This is the period immediately following *nakalu?ad* (late childhood). Physical changes noted during this period for females are the enlargement of the breasts, the coming of the menses, and the appearance of labial, axial, and pubic hair, as well as, for both sexes, the change in the voice. These changes come accompanied by an unusual appetite for food and desire for sleep. Most informants are agreed that during this period "all that one wants is to eat and sleep—the feeling is undescribable. One feels always tired and hungry." Waking up in the morning is a most trying task for many Malitbog pubescents.

Sociologically, the period of *supang* is characterized by marked self-consciousness; boys take particular note of their behavior, and girls are sensitive about their actions. Rufo's shyness near the girls was viewed by the adults as a sign of *supang.* He was always teased about it. Of course this self-consciousness is already defined and set in late childhood, especially in school. Sex differentiation among peers, which also starts during late childhood, becomes marked, and heterosexual companionship is openly discouraged. It is thus common to see boys go with boys and girls with girls; sometimes two boys are seen walking with hands locked and arms around each other's waist, or a girl is seen holding hands with another girl. An ideally accepted cultural behavior in Malitbog, this does not, as such behavior would be interpreted in many Western societies, reflect homosexual tendencies.

Growing intimacy characterizes the relationship between parents and children. A boy often accompanies his father in working in the fields, selling crops in the *poblacion,* and betting at the cockpit Sundays. He assists him in every activity, including sitting for him in card games. His father refers to him as ?*ang binangi*? *ko,* meaning "my right-hand man." Certain practices which were restricted to him in childhood are now allowed him. He can smoke and drink, and join older boys in serenading, although he may not start courting girls. In a word, he is initiated into the adult world by going with mature people and observing what they do. This is actually the period of apprenticeship.

The girls stay at home with the mother most of the time. Together, they launder, iron, and mend clothes, and gather vegetables in the field. They also cook the meals and work in the field together during planting and harvesting seasons. In this way the girls learn the skills of a good housewife. They are also taught proper behavior by their mothers. Giggling and showing of sexual aggressiveness is discouraged as "unbecoming of young girls." To be seen frequently alone with a boy in the field or on a lonely trail is discouraged because "people talk." Gossip can be twisted, and before long the girl loses her reputation.

CIRCUMCISION

Circumcision is the only rite which males undergo during the *supang,* and no elaborate ceremonies or sets of complex taboos are associated with it. It is also voluntary. Boys may group together and decide to undergo the operation, requesting a specialist for the purpose. There are two elderly men whom they patronize for the rite. Decisions to submit to circumcision are often reached by teasing prospective candidates and challenging their ability to withstand the pain of the operation.

I was among a group of five boys one hot noonday, resting under a jackfruit tree, when Indo, the oldest among the boys, started teasing Osi, the youngest, that "it is about time you are circumcised." Osi answered that it was not necessary, for he had heard his uncle say that Malitbog girls prefer uncircumcised men. Indo went on: "Ah, I do not believe you. You are just afraid—like the rest of the boys." There was a chorus of protest. "All right, if you are not afraid, let us go to Itek and be circumcised," he challenged the group. There were hesitations and protests. Osi finally said, "I will go if you will also be circumcised." The boys all agreed to go to

Sowing rice seeds over the cleared area.

Itek if Indo would submit to the operation. Afraid that he would be accused of being a coward himself, Indo said he would even be the first to undergo the cutting, "provided all of you follow afterwards." The rest agreed, and the five boys were circumcised that afternoon.

Ripe tomatoes, pork, and dried fish, among other foods, are avoided immediately after circumcision to prevent swelling of the penis. To treat the fresh wound, tender guava leaves are chewed and the spittle is applied to it before it is bandaged with a clean strip of cloth. To wash the wound every morning and evening until it is healed, a warm decoction of mature guava leaves is used.

Circumcision in early childhood is considered bad for the health. Moreover, a very young boy who is circumcised is made the object of the endless fun and ridicule of his playmates. The fact that he was circumcised in the hospital where he was born made Pedrito, the nephew of my host, very unhappy. Young boys his age would shout at the top of their voices whenever they saw him coming: *"Dyan dən si paltak, si paltak"* (Here comes the circumcised, the circumcised). Pedrito seldom joined the other boys of his age; he either played alone or with smaller boys and girls.

This ridicule develops in some boys a deep-seated fear of circumcision. The case of Ramon, a young boy of fourteen, best exemplifies this. Ramon went to work with Tio C. at the Reforestation Nursery in a nearby town. One day he went to join the other workers to bathe in the river. The men discovered that he was not yet circumcised. They teased him very roughly about it and later someone suggested that they better circumcise him, and should he resist the operation, they would have him hog-tied. This teasing went on for two days. Every time the men saw him they would say, *"ʔano turiʔən ta dən si Ramon?"* (Shall we circumcise Ramon now?). One man remarked that perhaps the best way to do it is when he is asleep. On hearing this, Ramon packed up his clothes and went home. When Tio C. later inquired why he left his job, Ramon said, "Because the men are determined to circumcise me if I remain there."

MENSTRUATION TABOOS

Pubescence among females is noted with the coming of the menses and the growing of the breasts. During its early phase, a girl is known as *malabatwanan,* a term derived from the root word *batwan,* a roundish, hard sour fruit of a tree of the same name. By this time the girl's nipples are hard and of the size of the *batwan.* While these physical changes are anticipated and accepted as inevitable, some girls say that they experience a feeling of awkwardness during the time when their bosoms first protrude and show.

There are certain practices which are observed with the first menses. As soon as the menstrual flow is felt and known, for example, a girl is told to go down a ladder, and on reaching the third step from below, to jump to the ground. Jumping over these steps is believed to influence the length of the menstrual periods; it will make the cycles normal. One informant said that his wife's menstrual cycle is rather long because "during the first day of her flow, she was so excited that she jumped over seven steps instead of three." The wife takes this comment good humoredly.

After jumping over these steps, a girl must take a sponge-bath every day. This is to condition her body to water so that during her later mensturations she can wash herself; otherwise, it will be dangerous for her even to drench her hair during her monthly "period." She will suffer pain all over her body, an ailment known as *pasmu*. Other prohibitions during menstruation include: (1) avoiding sour food, which will cause the girl to have an overflow and die; (2) refraining from hard work because this will stop the menstrual flow; and (3) taking a bath only on the fifth day after menstruation. Sweet food like porridge with sugar, candies, fruits, and the like are given to a girl in case she has difficulty during the first day of her menstruation.

Girls having their menstrual flow suffer no changes in their social or economic activities. They continue to do their everyday chores, except during the first day and when abdominal pain is severe. A girl may choose to stay in bed or be up and about in the house. However, during occasions when she is up, she helps in the kitchen, serves at the table, or baby-sits for a busy sibling. Also during her periods, she is not allowed to go to tobacco fields and gardens planted with beans and fruit trees, like cacao and breadfruits, because it is believed that during this time, a woman's body generates heat and strong odor, and should she go into these places, the flowers and leaves of the plants will wither, a phenomenon known as *lumpaw*.

HAMTUNG (ADOLESCENCE)

The best single point of reference for characterizing adolescence is advancing maturity. Although there is no serious concern over physiological maturity, which is accepted as part of growing up, there are noticeable modifications in the behavior of boys and girls. Adolescents are known as *hamtung*, full-grown persons. The parents are now on the lookout for prospective spouses for their children. Marriage is thought of and is possible quite early since most Malitbog youths are out of school. There are only two young girls and one boy who were in the high school during the time I was doing fieldwork in 1964–1965.

The most important change during this period is the structuring of definitive sex roles in the adult phase of community activities. As already noted, sex differentiation starts during puberty, but as adolescence comes, a corpus of other normative elements are introduced into the behavioral pattern; among these are particularity of sex and consciousness of status based on age. Adolescent boys are supposed to do manly work, the girls, feminine tasks. Joking patterns change and older boys are regarded by their younger siblings with respect and admiration.

Male dominance begins to be emphasized within the sibling group. This is partly due to the fact that the adolescent boy takes practically one-half of the father's actual job in the field. He is now considered an important contributor to the family larder; thus other younger siblings are told to obey him. On some occasions he is even consulted by the parents in major decisions affecting the welfare of the family. Older female siblings act as mother surrogates, but their voice in matters of importance to the family is secondary to that of their brothers. In a word, adolescence is conceived in Malitbog as a period in point of time when individuals, in the performance of their respective roles, respond to a combination of puberty norms and adult expectations. Young men and women participate in adult activities, as well as in some of the affairs of the younger people such as ball games, but in a very different order from those of married persons or of pubescents.

An adolescent female is known as *daraga,* meaning a full-grown woman, and an adolescent male, as *?ulitawo,* meaning a full-grown man. Social roles of both sexes involve important elements of restraint, both in behavior and language. Modesty is the rule among girls, and conscientiousness, among boys. The intimate companionship among peer groups begins to break up as males and females become more and more involved, economically, in the task of supporting the family.

THE *DARAGA*

Because a *daraga* is capable of bearing a child, she is always warned by the mother or older kin to be careful about her relationship with boys. She is much coveted now for her readiness for marriage, and every boy would try his luck; thus sexual "experimentation" can occur, and if she loses her virginity, she automatically loses her chances of marrying a good man. In a society where chastity is the primary criterion for selecting a wife, any girl whose morals are suspect is courted only for sexual adventures, not for establishing a permanent home. A "fallen" girl does not suffer alone since she automatically ruins the reputation of her family. Thus adolescent girls are not allowed to go about the barrio unchaperoned.

Domestic training is given particular attention, and qualities which will make a good housewife are further emphasized. An adolescent girl who becomes clumsy with her work is admonished by her mother with the words: "If you were married early, you would have several grandchildren by now and yet you do not know how to work well." The words are intended to shame and remind the girl who, having grown up, must know her responsibilities.

Girls openly discuss the opposite sex only when there are no males around; it is considered unbecoming to talk about sex or marriage in their presence. Thus as soon as a brother or male relative comes around, they shift the topic to something else. They are more restricted in their behavior than boys. At ages 16 and 17 they are no longer permitted to sleep in their friends' houses.

THE *?ULITAWO*

The *?ulitawo* enjoys more privilege than the *daraga.* Their mobility is not as restricted as the latter's. In fact, they are expected to be about the barrio, working the fields either alone or in groups, doing odd jobs in the *poblacion,* serenading at night or spending time with their peer groups. This privilege accorded to *?ulitawo* is based on the consensus that "once a man is a man," meaning that there is no moral risk involved in a man's mobility, unlike that of a girl, whose readiness for marriage is the object of the male's sexual adventures. When Mal-am Angi's wife complained about their son's passing the night with his friends in Sitio Agsiw, her husband curtly said, "He is not a woman that you should keep him here. Moreover, nothing will be lost—turn him upside down he is still a man."

This statement reflects the views of many of the Malitbog people and explains why mothers are more strict with their daughters than with their sons. While chastity is emphasized as the criterion for the choice of a wife, a male expressedly wants to achieve sexual adventures. In a small barrio, of course, sex adventures do not usually go beyond stolen kisses along the way or a few passes during short privileged moments. Parents and other older kin are always around to prevent anything scandalous from happening. Boys, however, brag about their sex adventures, and this is the favorite topic of many conversations.

Parents are not strict with boys because as grown-up members of the family they share with their father the responsibility of supporting the family. Thus wider latitude is allowed them in their activities. Restrictions are imposed only when boys come home drunk nights or when they become involved in petty crimes or other misdemeanors. To be drunk occasionally is not sanctioned against; but when drinking become habitual and excessive, it is undesirable. Also, a known drunkard loses his chances of winning a pretty girl. This is one form of social control, and parents emphasize this when calling the young man's attention to his unacceptable behavior.

Discipline during adolescence does not involve physical punishment, as during childhood. In fact, to upbraid a young man in public is considered unnecessary and bad. Parents and adult members of the family note this carefully, because young men are deemed to be dangerous when provoked; their tempers are not easily controlled. The case of a young man who stabbed his father to death during a baptismal party in 1960 was still fresh in the memory of the people in 1964. The young man was said to be drunk at the time and was creating trouble at the gathering. His father scolded him in public, telling him to go home and sleep. Without much ado, the young man unsheathed his knife (the *pinuti*?) and stabbed his father in the stomach. The old man died right away. Notwithstanding the concensus of opinion that the young man was at fault, some also blamed the father for what happened. "He could have called the boy aside and talked to him instead of lashing at him right then and there," some people commented when the case was narrated to me.

An important modification in the boy's social role during adolescence is his greater participation in adult activities like sitting in the barrio council, serving as the barrio policeman, and participating in reciprocal labor. He is looked upon as mature enough to assume certain responsibilities well. Parents always enjoin their sons to keep away from trouble. While it is fun to watch children quarrel and fight —in fact they are encouraged to do so because bravery is held as one of the highest norms in the barrio—it is not the case with adolescent boys. They are admonished to be careful not to be involved in any fight. This concern is due to the fact that fighting among the grown-ups leads to fatalities. "When someone wields a knife, no one runs away" one informant explained, "That is why fighting among adults is serious." In spite of this injunction, occasional fights occur, especially during festivities and other gatherings.

SOCIAL PARTICIPATION

Division of labor is re-emphasized and clearly defined during the adolescent years. On the farm, the girls do light tasks like planting and harvesting; heavier ones like plowing, harrowing, and hauling are the boys' responsibilities. Occasionally, the girls may tend to the carabaos, goats, and cows, but the greater part of their work schedule is at home—cooking, taking care of the siblings, feeding the chickens and pigs, and laundering the clothes. The men are expected to fetch water and chop firewood, but women do these tasks when work schedules in the field are tight.

On such occasions as barrio dances, baptismal and wedding parties, and religious celebrations adolescent boys and girls do not mix. The girls situate themselves in one corner and the boys in another. Any socializing between them is limited to male chaperones, who are mostly relatives or siblings. The permission of a girl's male chaperone is first asked if a boy wants to dance with her. The girl's reaction is one of careful restraint. She looks up to her chaperone, who gives her the sign whether to accept or reject the invitation. In accepting, the girl stands up without even looking at the boy, and follows him to the dance floor. The girl stiffens a little when she is held by the boy; to relax and enjoy the dance may be interpreted by the spectators as "unwomanly." In many cases dancing is simply walking around, swaying from side to side. Occasional conversations may take place; often the partners do not even smile at each other. The scene becomes entirely different if the girl dances with her chaperone or with her cousins and siblings. Here the partners are relaxed and their steps are danced to the tempo of the music. The introduction of modern dances has raised many eyebrows among some old folk, although there are equally a number of them who agree that "it is fun to watch." Even in performing these dances, where partners do not hold hands, a girl is still expected to show some restraint in wiggling her hips or shaking her entire body, if her partner is not a relative or a sitio-mate.

7 / Courtship and marriage

T HE HIGHEST ASPIRATIONS of most Malitbog youths are to win a spouse, to have children, and to live independently. Few say that their ambition is to seek employment in the city and that marriage is a hindrance to this ambition. Though equally shared by both sexes, winning a spouse as a goal is more explicit among men than among women. Being a spinster is not considered shameful. In fact, one of the favorite arguments of young women in refusing an unfavored suitor is: "*Mala?on takən* [I have decided to become a spinster]." In spite of this view, there are no spinsters in Malitbog. On the other hand, being a bachelor for a long time is viewed as ridiculous. The man is regarded as abnormal; something is wrong with him. Thus he is often the object of village fun. He is teased roughly and is given such derogatory nicknames as *?agi?* (effeminate), *warat buras* (without genitals), *matalaw* (coward; reference is made to approaching girls), and *wa?at ?itlug* (without testicles). In spite of this strong sanction against remaining a bachelor, there are bachelors in the barrio who are past their forties.

The second reason why winning a mate is weighted more heavily and expressed more explicitly by men is the fact that women are expected to be demure, even about courtship. It is the men who are expected to initiate courtship. Because under the barrio norm girls simply wait to be courted, to initiate courtship is to make them morally censurable. Thus to be noticed, visited, serenaded, and eventually courted is the fond dream of many Malitbog girls. It is indeed a prize to aspire toward, for to be courted is to be honored in that courtship is regarded by all as a public affirmation that the girl possesses good moral character, beauty, charm, and other desirable virtues. It is the most exciting phase in a woman's life.

There are married women, however, who are said to have initiated courtship, and the people have low moral regard for them. To characterize a bold attempt on the part of a woman to make the first move in courtship, they use the term *kalamay* (to sugar); hence, the act of winning one's way into a man's heart. This is frowned upon by most women: "Women with good reputation will never do it. Only the flirts do it." The term for flirts is *?uragan,* and girls thus characterized are conceived to have longer clitoris than normal women. This accounts for their sexual aggressiveness.

The idea of love and courtship begins early among the youth, especially in school. In group games, both in school and outside of the schoolground, boys and girls are paired by their playmates. This introduces them to the idea of love and partnership. Sometimes this develops into closer relationship which culminates in adolescent years into actual courtship and eventually marriage. On the 20 marriages which took place since 1955, 12 started in the school.

COURTSHIP PATTERN

Normally, courtship begins when the boy becomes an ʔ*ulitawo* and the girl, a *daraga*. This is about a year following the period of puberty and in the beginning of adolescence for both. During this period, the ʔ*ulitawo*, as indicated earlier, takes active part in various community affairs. He plows the field, pastures and bathes the carabao, plants, harvests, and threshes rice, and does other work with his peers, some of whom have been his childhood playmates. During rest hours the favorite topic of jokes and serious conversations is girls. Here the ʔ*ulitawo* learns who is the new arrival in the barrio, who is courting whom, what kind of a girl so and so is. The traits of practically all known girls in the barrio are talked about. It is during this peer group discussion that an ʔ*ulitawo* forms an idea about a certain *daraga,* or decides to take a second look at the quick-tongued little girl with whom he quarreled most of the time in school during their childhood days. As Loreto says of his wife: "When we were studying, we quarreled almost every day. The other children, you see, had paired us and she did not like the idea. Everytime we were teased she hit me with a stick. Oh! we sort of hated each other. Perhaps it is our luck—we ended as husband and wife."

Malitbog residents believe in luck, which is known locally as *badlit ka palad* (written on the person's palm), *suherti* (luck), *signus* (signs of time), and *sukud* (fate). Even if the man and the woman love each other very much, if it is not their luck or fate, they would not get married. Certain circumstances would befall either one and prevent the union from taking place. Thus, informants would always cite the case of Honorio and Pedrita, whose wedding had already been prepared. On the morning of the scheduled date, Pedrita eloped with someone she had known but for a week. When I interviewed Honorio, he was no longer bitter. "I used to be bitter about it, but not anymore. I guess it is our *sukud.* I would have been unhappy had I married her, who knows?" Honorio married Pedrita's younger sister.

Among the various occasions which provide Malitbog youth with the chance to meet girls or to renew acquaintances with childhood playmates are: the planting and harvesting of staple food crops, town fiestas, barrio dances, ball games during weekends, *belasyon* (wakes for the dead), baptismal and marriage parties, funerals, and so on. Recent additions to these local events are religious activities connected with the Protestant church work. Aside from Sunday morning services, for example, there are prayer meetings every Thursday and visitations during Sunday afternoons. Most of the recruits for these activities are the ʔ*ulitawo* and the *daraga.* They go around the barrio together. This "togetherness" oftentimes blossoms into love affairs.

To initiate courtship a boy picks out among the prospects, and together with his friends visits the girl of his choice. Visiting hours are usually in the evenings, although others do it on Sunday afternoons. The first visit is followed by a *harana* (serenade); sometimes it precedes the latter. The reason why friends are invited to come along during the initial visits is that the young suitor does not feel confident about his ability to carry on the suit. Moreover, the friends act as appraisers. Immediately after leaving the girl's house, the suitor asks his friends to comment: "*ʔano ba?* [What now?]." If the comment is favorable, the suit is pressed; otherwise, the girl is dropped and another one is scouted for. If the suitor insists on pressing for a love affair with a girl most of his peers do not approve of, he becomes their laughingstock. His gangmates will always drop comments which make him unhappy. In a word, peer-group consensus functions as a mechanism for social control, an enforcer of group norms.

The case of Justo exemplifies this behavior among peer groups in Malitbog. I was with a group of five teen-age boys who were watching carabaos one afternoon. They were talking about the young female harvesters who arrived from the neighboring town. As Justo approached the group, Julian, the oldest in the group, coughed a little and said in a loud voice: "Did anyone see the sweet potato I found yesterday? Ah, it was nice looking, but full of *balantik* [small holes caused by worms]." The boys laughed. They knew what he meant. Bernie, Justo's cousin, stood up and said: "Perhaps you dug it up with eyes closed. Or was it nighttime when you found it?" There was another burst of laughter. Everyone knew that Justo was courting one of the new girls. He had requested Julian to accompany him to visit the girl. The latter rated the girl poorly, but Justo thought "she was pretty and fair complexioned." The joke about the sweet potato was repeated as Justo joined the group. He understood what his gangmates were talking about. He slowly walked away, without saying anything. The following morning he announced to the group: "Well, I canceled that girl out of my prospects for this harvest season. *Kasi,* you made fun of her. Also, I went back to her boardinghouse last night to take a second look and I agree with you, boys: she looks like a jackfruit—too many pimples."

Serenading is slowly losing its popularity among the contemporary youth. It is used occasionally during the harvest season when girls from other barrios come to help harvest the palay. Young boys group together and serenade the fairest among the newcomers. The males among the newcomers also band together, befriend the local boys, and serenade the fairest among the Malitbog girls. In a word, the harvest season provides the occasion for both groups—the newcomer and the local youths—to meet and initiate courtship and marriage. If no one among the unmarried boys plays the guitar, they request a married man who can play to come along. Because serenading during this season is fun, a number of married men usually come along and help facilitate things for the unmarried boys.

The most favored hour for the serenade is midnight. Sometimes the boys give advance notice to the girls about their coming. A joust of songs, known as *bangiʔanay,* features the serenade. In the contest, the boy proposes love and the girl discourages him from pursuing it. The one who first runs out of songs is declared the loser. The news about the serenade often spreads around the barrio immediately the following day and the best singer gains barrio-wide reputation.

The girl whose name was mentioned by the serenaders is teased by friends about it: "Oy, oy, somebody got serenaded last night." Teasing often starts a courtship. Even if the persons concerned participated in the serenade for fun, they soon get ideas about each other, because the teasers talk about them. To be angry or to show offense for being teased and paired is bad taste; people do not think highly of those who cannot take and enjoy jokes. They are known as *pikun,* a derogatory term meaning "bad tempered; short-roped individuals."

If a boy is well received by the girl's family in subsequent visits after the serenade, he formalizes the courtship. He visits the girl alone. He also informs his gangmates not to court the girl because he has his eyes on her. Even if one of the friends had previously entertained a feeling for the same girl, he usually withdraws in favor of the one who is first to tell the group about his feelings. In this way, rivalry is minimized. Thus, it was only after Flor was married that Uling, her mother, knew that Erning, the boy she wanted for her daughter, had an eye on the girl. When asked why he kept silent, Erning said that Emit, Flor's husband, revealed his feelings to the group ahead of him. "It is shameful to court Flor when everybody knows that Emit is also courting her," Erning reasoned." He left Malitbog on the day Flor was married.

While conformity to peer-group norms is closely observed, there are also cases of deviations from it. Quarrels and, sometimes, fatal incidents arise from nonobservance of the rule. For example, Ramon, the son of Mal-am Inggo, the carpenter, was mauled and stabbed by Berting, the fiance of Simona, a lovely lass from Sitio Agsiw. Ramon, according to the story that circulated in the barrio later, had warned Berting to "stop bothering Simona because I am courting her." However, Berting did not listen; he continued visiting the girl. One evening Ramon waited for him at the dark section of the trail after he visited Simona and belted him with a plow chain. When Berting resisted, he was stabbed. Ramon escaped to Mindanao and was not heard from since then.

As soon as a boy visits a girl more than once, her parents and older siblings start to be watchful over the developing affair. The mother sees to it that she is around during every visit; if she has an important engagement, she leaves one of the siblings to keep the sister company. If the boy is liked, no one comments on the affair; if not, he is confronted rather rudely about his intentions by the girl's parents and her siblings. They ask him about his ability to support a wife, where and how he earns a living, who are his relatives, and so on. These questions are actually unnecessary because often the girl's family knows all about the boy; nevertheless, these are asked in order to embarrass him. Frequently the boy does not return.

In revealing his intentions to the girl, the boy does not speak about it directly. He resorts to linguistic maneuvers, locally known as *pabati?bati?*. He tells her, for example, how sorry he is for getting her to be the talk of everybody because of his frequent visits. If the girl says she does not mind, then he speaks of his love. Even if the girl likes the boy, she is not supposed to answer him right away. She must pretend to be offended by his boldness in mentioning love, saying that she thought all along that his visits were for friendship and not for serious matters like love. The boy must continue pleading until the girl answers him positively. The reason behind this romantic strategy was expressed by Buday, a much-sought-after girl in the barrio: "In this way you will know how sincere the man is. Men have many colors, you know. We girls have to be careful. Look at Marta. What happened to her because she was not careful. Bha! people talk."

Even if the parents like the boy, they maintain extra care that nothing happens to their daughters before marriage. To prevent any sexual experimentation, the girl is armed by them with charms consisting of dried *huya? huya?* (a kind of plant) leaves, scrapings from the mortar, and pieces of shells of dryland snails. These are wrapped with a piece of cloth and worn as an amulet by the girl; sometimes these are sewn to the seam of her dress. According to informants, the *huya? huya?* will make the boy shy, the mortar scrapings will make him stay put where he sits, and the pieces of shells will make him move slowly like a snail. Others say that the charms have the power to make the man's genitalia weak, hence incapable of sexual intercourse.

Many boys anticipate this *panapat* (the act of wearing charms), so they also use countercharms to win the girls' affection. One of these charms Malitbog youths use is known as *lumay.* It consists of leaves, roots, and scrapings from unknown plants mixed with coconut oil. Should the boy succeed in applying this concoction on the hair of the desired girl, "she will go crazy for you; she is yours for the asking." *Hiwit* (sorcery) is another popular method of winning a girl's hand; it can also be used for attracting men. If a man wants a particular girl and she is in love with another man, he secures part of her clothes and boils it. He keeps this material boiling in the pot until the girl comes to him. The *tiw·tiw* is another charm used to win a girl's affection. This is losing popularity among the contemporary youths. In this case, a man secures certain roots of plants prescribed by a *baylan* (medium healer) and locates himself at the upper part of the stream where the girl goes bathing. Then he soaks the paraphernalia into the water. As soon as the girl pours the contaminated water over her head, she loses her reason and "she follows the man wherever he goes, come what may." Sometimes the possessor of the *tiw·tiw* pounds the roots and squeezes the juice into the well where the girl takes a bath, and obtains the same results.

Courtship need not end in matrimony. A number of factors are considered before a suitor presses for marriage. Age is one of these. The ideal age for boys is 20 or above; for the girls, 18 or above. By the age of 20 the boy is considered mature and is capable of supporting a family. How much money or rice he has accumulated is another consideration. If he has not saved anything, the girl's parents usually discourage the match. The qualities which girls should possess in order to be desirable are: industry, modesty, and good public relations, especially in dealing with the prospective in-laws. The same criteria hold true for the boys. Beauty and good looks are a bonus, but not important in selecting a wife or husband. Place of residence is considered important by many parents.

MARRIAGE

Marriage, known locally as *kasal,* is the culmination of courtship and romance. A married couple is known as *kasado* and the nuclear family established by them is known as *minyu?.* To be married is to be treated as an adult, irrespective of one's biological age. Perhaps it is because of responsibilities inherent in married life that the acceptance of the once carefree boys and girls into the adult world of Malitbog is hastened. Marriage is conceived of in the barrio as a sacred bond that unites a man and a woman into a permanent, lifelong partnership. It confers to both husband and wife the exclusive right to sexual relations, to have offspring, and to establish an independent family unit. Monogamy is the rule. The provisions of the laws of the Republic of the Philippines, which do not permit divorce, are applicable in Malitbog. Legal separation is permitted, although remarriage resulting therefrom is not considered legal. Adultery and concubinage are frowned upon. The death of either spouse is the only permissible excuse for remarriage. In any case, however, the widow or widower, even after the second marriage, is still obligated to support his children by the first marriage and to celebrate the anniversaries of the departed spouse, especially during the first day of November.

Aside from establishing privileged relations between husband and wife, marriage functions in Malitbog as a cultural mechanism through which alliances between families are formed for economic security, mutual protection in time of danger, and local social prestige. The latter is not as sought after as the two former. In a word, the institution of marriage is one way of fashioning certain relationships designed to meet individual and group needs and goals.

Barrio *endogamy* (that is, marriage within the barrio itself) is much preferred, although no formal rules restricting *exogamy* (that is, marriage outside of the barrio) exist. Among the reasons given by the people why barrio endogamy is preferred are: (1) "We are not certain about the character of people from other barrios. They might be *ʔaswang* [witches], *masalʔag* [negligent], and lazy." (2) "Marrying within the barrio is preferable because we know all about the girls and boys. If a spouse is a stranger, it is difficult to adjust to him. Also, the inheritance will not spread to other people."

Because of barrio endogamy, cousin marriages have been predominant. First- and second-cousin marriages are considered good, but third-cousin marriages are said to be bad. They are known as *nagakurus* (cross) and are accordingly considered *masarut* (fraught with dangers). The old folks always point to the case of Nardo, who married his third cousin, Maya. They had two invalid children. This belief in numerology is so strong and pervasive in the barrio that even preparations for and setting the date of the marriage are made to suit certain fortunate numbers.

MARRIAGE ARRANGEMENTS

Pabagtiʔ As soon as the girl's parents are informed of the boy's real intentions, a meeting between both sets of parents is arranged. This is known as *pabagtiʔ* (a similar occasion is known as *padolʔong* in other parts of Panay island). Its main purpose is for the boy's kin group to find out whether or not the other kin group has promised the girl in marriage to someone else. Of course everybody knows what goes on in a small community and, from the standpoint of an outsider, the *pabagtiʔ* is unnecessary. The meeting, nevertheless, is held as though this were not the case. The *pabagtiʔ* may also be viewed as the first public announcement to all and sundry that "this girl has been sought." Henceforth, the other boys must desist from courting the girl; anyone who insists takes the risk of antagonizing not only the kinsmen of the accepted suitor but also the relatives of the girl, who are expected to honor their words during the *pabagtiʔ*. In spite of these restrictions, the girl is free to change her mind. I have no report, however, of a case in which this has happened in the past. Actually, the *pabagtiʔ* is not usually held unless a girl has already accepted the man; nonetheless, it is the consensus among Malitbog people that the woman has the final say and can change her mind if she likes to.

No agreement relative to the forthcoming marriage is reached during the *pabagti?*. The girl's parents normally bid for time to consider the matter and to talk it over with the older members of their kin group. A date is scheduled for a second meeting, known as *pahimpit*. This is to ascertain whether the woman's family favors the match or not.

The second meeting, as before, involves feasting and drinking. It is a little more elaborate than the *pabagti?*. The members of the boy's family bring to the girl's house a quantity of foods. These are cooked and served to those who come to witness and participate in the ceremony. Each family selects a spokesman to represent it in the battle of wits regarding the boy's proposal of marriage. The parents of either the boy or the girl cannot, by this time, act as their respective spokesmen because it is believed that if they do, they will feel rheumatic pains in the knees. Likewise, the boy's party should leave at once after the discussion, even if the meeting lasts until the wee hours of the morning. It is taboo for them to sleep in the prospective bride's house.

Metaphoric language is used to state indirectly but beautifully the purpose of the second meeting. The boy's party confronts the girl's group once more. In this meeting the two spokesmen—representing the contending parties—engage in a battle of wit. Thus when Tio C., the popular *manugsiday* (that is, one who is well versed in marriage poetry), acted as spokesman for his nephew, he opened the "negotiation" in this manner (addressing the old man from the girl's side): "While we were walking in the field, some hills away, we were attracted to the fragrant smell of a flower. The scent came from this direction. We followed it and true enough we are here in your place. We would like to acquire a bud of this rare possession of yours."

The spokesman of the girl replied: "We do not have any flower here. You must have made a mistake. It could have been the scent of flowers from other gardens. Our garden had been bare for a long time now. The tender buds of our roses have been plucked away two summers ago." Tio C. countered: "You cannot hide these things. We are certain the fragrance comes from your garden. Even if you keep the flower inside the altar room, its scent will still stir the neighborhood, just as incense fills the room when someone performs the rite. You are not telling the truth. How much would you want us to pay for it?"

This battle of wit continues for several hours. The boy's spokesman now makes a demand for a definite answer. As in the first meeting, the girl's family bids for time and asks the boy's family to return within a week or two.

Padol?ong   The third meeting is known as *padol?ong*. The boy is formally presented to the family and kin of the girl. The following account typifies a *padol?-ong* ceremony observed in 1964.

Upon arrival in the field, I was informed that Roming, son of Mal-am Ingo and prospective husband of Maret, daughter of Tio Casyano, was scheduled to be presented to the girl's kin group. Two weeks before, all the relatives of Tio Casyano and Tia Puring were informed of the event, since to ignore them was to provoke

Marriage plans are sealed by a ceremony participated in by the members of the boy's kin group and the girl's close relatives.

their anger and would start gossip in the barrio. Everyone made a comment or two about the prospective bride and groom. Some of the comments were favorable; some were not. Nevertheless, no single opinion from either family or kin group was heard that prevented the celebration of the *padol?ong*. In fact, every family head present contributed either his share of food and money or moral support to the entire kin group.

Foods were brought to the house of the prospective bride in the morning of the day set for the meeting. These were cooked for lunch. After everybody had eaten, parts of the foods reserved for the ceremony were brought into the middle of the house. The cooked meat, fish, and other dishes were placed on a bamboo tray, covered with fresh banana leaves. The *tuba?* (coconut beverage) was also brought in. Two spokesmen, each representing both kin groups, placed themselves opposite each other, at both ends of the prepared foods. The oldest member of one group stood up and filled two empty glasses with *tuba,* giving one to each of the two spokesmen. The latter exchanged glasses to assure all that "they can relax and enjoy the affair because the food is not poisoned."

The exchange of drinks was followed by the *timbalya* or poetic joust, which lasted for several hours. I was told that the *timbalya* could drag deep into the night if both spokesmen were skillful. Malitbog barrio folk love and have high regard for poets and orators. The following examples typify the *timbalya* joust.

Spokesman for the girl: [Free translation]

> *Pangkut ?aku pasin?o*   This, I would like to ask
> *Hangəd ?aku nabərəng*   For I am bewildered
> *Hangəd gid natingala*   I am greatly puzzled
> *?anu balang kastaha*   What are the reasons
> *?anu nga ?isturaha?*   The meaning behind all these?
> *?insa nagdarapit kaw*   Why did you bring
> *Ka nakən ?it pagka?on?*   Into my house lots of food?

Spokesman for the boy:

> *?indi ka lang kaday mabərəng*   Do not be alarmed
> *?indi ka matingala*   Do not be puzzled
> *Ka darapit kong pagka?on*   Why I brought the food
> *?idara kong tagyamən*   Why I brought the drinks.
> *Ngani dinapit ?aku sa langbən*   I came here to your house
> *?ada? man sa lilingdən*   I dared your domain
> *Darapit ku kayay galang*   With highest respect
> *Dara kuy ?ala ?ala*   With serious thoughts
> *?ulayhun sa pamangkut*   For I intend to ask you
> *Langkuy sa pagpasin ?o*   I intend really to inquire
> *Hay may ginararip ?akung dəmdəm* I am looking for something
> *May ginasagap ?uriman.*   Something dear to the heart.

Then the boy's representative spoke about a lost bird which he and his companions were looking for; then he shifted to the sound of gongs which they heard and recognized as their lost instrument and which they wanted back. He ended with the proposal for marriage.

Panghagad If the boy is accepted, he starts serving the girl's family for a period of time, which may mean weeks or months before the date set for the wedding. This is the time, some of the informants say, when the man's true character is observed, although this is not actually necessary, because the boy, if he comes from the barrio, is already known to the family of the girl. If he is not known, it is too late to reject him even if the prospective in-laws do not like him because they have already committed themselves. In Malitbog a man's word is his honor. I do not know of a case in which a man was rejected for having been found to be no good during the *panghagad*. Moreover, every man always puts his best foot forward during this period.

In the olden days, the *panghagad* lasted for several years. Local stories tell that in those days young Malitbog suitors were required to work for about seven years with the prospective bride's family, wearing out within this period a number of pestles, and at least one mortar. Pounding rice and helping in the fields were the major work requirements then. Today this is no longer observed. The *panghagad* lasts for a few weeks only, at most a month.

Palista A few weeks before the scheduled wedding day, both families of the boy and the girl go to the *poblacion* to apply for a marriage contract. A spokesman, usually the barrio captain or anyone with "contacts" at the municipal building, comes along in order to facilitate the application. After being signed by both parents, indicating their consent to the union, and by the boy and the girl, the contract is submitted to the treasurer, who posts notices of the forthcoming marriage at the municipal hall or at the market place. If no one contests the announcement within ten days, a marriage license is issued to the contracting parties.

From the municipal hall, the parties proceed to the church to arrange the wedding date with the church *fiscal* (secretary) and to clear with him the type of wedding desired—that is, special or *yano* (ordinary). Arrangements for the reading of the ban every Sunday is also taken up with him. As soon as everything is fixed, the couple is brought to the priest for an interview which is usually limited to their knowledge about prayers. If one of the couples does not know how to pray, the priest sends for a relative or for the sponsor to help him with the necessary prayer.

Kasal The wedding follows the *palista,* locally known as *kasal*. As soon as everything is set and on the eve of the wedding, all the kinsmen of both parties come to the house where the festivity is to be held, normally at the house of the girl's parents. Pigs, carabaos, and other livestock are butchered during the evening, cut up, and prepared for cooking in the morning. Fowls are dressed in the morning. Minor feasting starts in the evening as some of the men cook meat as *sumsuman* (appetizer) and other foods for supper. Practically all members of the kin groups come to help. The women prepare the kitchen for use, check the dishes and other things necessary for the feast. The preparation for the nuptial ceremony and the *punsyun* (feast) which follows continues into the morning. As soon as everything is ready, the men and women take a short nap. By the third crowing of the cocks (about 3:00 A.M.) they wake up and start to cook and to prepare to go to town.

Two people are chosen to manage the affair. The one appointed in over-all charge of the festivity is usually the oldest male member, and the one who takes care of the bride and the groom is the oldest female member of the groups. An acquaintance in the town is usually requested to allow his house to be used by the groom and the bride for dressing, since it is impractical to dress in the barrio—their clothes would be soiled. The bride is assisted by her sisters, mother, and close relatives; the groom, by his brothers and other relatives. Together the groups go to the church. During the marriage ceremony, the man steps over the feet of the woman as soon as the priest starts to bless them—an act done to make the woman subservient to the man. It is believed that should this not be done, the man will be under the woman's dominance. Another practice is for both to close their eyes as the ring is being placed— to make them surmount all difficulties in married life. Finally, and as the veil is placed on the couple, the man must press the left hand of the bride with his right hand—to make the wife agreeable to all the man's wishes and to achieve harmony in the home.

After the ceremony, the newlyweds and their retinues pose for photographs. In former days there was a *sinulug* (bolo dance) which followed as soon as the couple stepped out of the church. In the house, they proceed to the family altar built in one of the corners of the *sala,* after having been congratulated by those whom they passed by on the way. Here they light the candles, kneel, and pray. After praying, one of the older members of the boy's family steps forward and gives the newly-weds the "gift"—a certain amount of money—to start them off. Then the bride rises and kisses her mother and other relatives. The crying session among the women starts. The groom shakes hands with friends and acquaintances who gather around him. The bride retires and changes her dress for the feast. Dancing may or may not start right away, although drinking and feasting may well have been going on. The *punsyon* starts as soon as the guests arrive. It is interesting to note that no vegetables, except breadfruit and some leaves that go with the meat, are served during the *punsyon.* To serve vegetables is to lower the family prestige. Dishes are generally made of *pansit* (noodles), *putsiru* (meat cooked with ripe bananas and sweet potatoes), and *arroz a la valenciana* (Spanish rice dish) and other viands.

Pasakaʔ ka ʔumagad   The night following the wedding, the couple sleep separately, as it is believed that if they do sleep together, one of them will be sickly throughout life. Some people, however, think that this taboo is fast being laid aside. The next morning, the groom brings his bride to the house of his parents. The boy's family prepares a simple reception for the new daughter-in-law and for some close relatives who come along. This is known as *pasakaʔ ka ʔumagad* (to welcome the in-law). Marriage is sexually consummated during the second night in the man's house, although many of my young informants state, "We do not observe that anymore." The following morning the boy's family accompanies the newly weds and returns the girl to her parents' place, where she and her husband will stay for a year. Another reception is prepared.

Initial matrilocal residence is the pattern among most Malitbog residents. It is part of the wedding requirements, and I doubt whether it is a residence rule in that departure from it is possible if (1) the husband is an only son; (2) the girl's family is large; (3) the husband is well off. Economic considerations seem to be the guide for residence rules. After the initial matrilocal residence the couple establish their own home, either near the parents' house or sitio of the wife or near the boy's parents in their sitio; there is no strict regulation on the matter. Most Malitbog families live neolocally, away from their residence of orientation before marriage.

8 / Family and household

A FTER MARRIAGE, Malitbog youths are viewed quite differently by other members of the community. Before this event, they are regarded as "unreliable" individuals, even if they are productively involved in supporting the family. Marriage is the turning point. Most informants are agreed that "as soon as a man establishes a family of his own, he can be relied upon for so many things. He will think twice before doing anything bad." Badong, the former village bully, was always referred to as an example in illustrating this point. "Look at him," informants would tell me. "Before marriage, *susmariosep*,[1] he was the most irresponsible man in the barrio. He was the number-one drunk, gambler, and troublemaker. But after marriage, he is a changed man. He keeps away from troubles and has become what one could call 'the ideal husband.' "

In other words, bringing up a family is an important element of socialization. The change in status automatically brings about certain changes in expectations of people and in the performances of roles of those concerned. Some of the previously held values are dropped, new norms are developed, and some practices are no longer followed. To a child, who witnesses all of these events, this shift in expectations and role performances among adults is crucial to his learning process. He begins to understand, empirically, "what bringing up a family" means as he sees his fun-loving sibling become a serious-minded family man. He starts to have fuller grasp of in-law problems, residence pattern, authority, adult obligations, kinship relations, and so on. He knows, by listening and watching, what people might expect of him when he grows up like his newlywed sibling, cousin, or neighbor.

Because much of what a child learns takes place within the family circle, it is important that its nature and function as a mechanism for socialization be described. In this way, we may be able to assess adequately the process of growing up in the barrio.

THE FAMILY

Almost all Malitbog residents are agreed that the family is the basic social, economic, political, and religious unit of their society. In its elementary form, this unit is composed of the father, the mother, and their unmarried children, either naturally

---

[1] From an expression *Jesus, Maria y Jose.*

born to them or adopted by them. The local concept of the family, commonly referred to as *pamilya* (Spanish, *familia*) includes members who are out of residence, provided they are not married. Children holding jobs outside of the barrio, where they stay either temporarily or permanently, continue to visit their parents and help support the younger siblings. This duty is stressed by the parents as part of the children's obligations in adult life. Typical examples are two of the children of Ambo who have jobs in Manila, the former capital city of the Philippines. They have been living in the city since 1959 and intend to live there permanently, but they have regularly sent money to their parents for the support of the family and they come home at least once a year.

The strong framework of reciprocal rights and duties existing among the members of the family is also extended to include obligations to neighbors. There is no geographical limit which defines the neighborhood circumference. In terms of action processes, however, it can be deduced from the day-to-day activities. For example, one defines his neighbors as those persons or families with whom his family exchanges food, to whom they go in time of need, irrespective of whether or not these persons live within calling distance or have moved away, who can be visited without formal rituals or previous notice, and who interact with his own family in friendly and familiar terms.

The Malitbog family is monogamous. Concubinage or the *querida* complex, apparently predominant in some areas of Panay, is absent in the barrio. This is probably due to (1) the presence of a belief that a union not sanctioned by the church (Protestant or Catholic) brings misfortune to both male and female, and (2) the fact that practically everyone knows everybody in the barrio and any sign of infidelity on the part of either the husband or the wife is likely to be known right away. Moreover, the members of the group whose security is endangered by the bad luck accruing from such an act will not tolerate such a condition to exist in the community, and they rally against the adulterous individuals, pressuring them into correcting the wrong and falling in line with what is accepted as right.

The case of Benig and Sepa exemplifies this group concern. Benig was married to Juanita for seven years. They had five children. During the harvest season of 1965, Benig met and fell in love with Sepa, one of the female harvesters who came to Malitbog for the season. Before harvest time was over, rumors went around the barrio that Benig and Sepa were seen by several persons making love near the brook. This angered the old folk. One evening a group of old men came to Benig and confronted him about the rumor. At first, Benig denied the affair but when witnesses were called, he admitted having an affair with Sepa. "She gave me all the opportunities, why should I not take advantage of them? I am a man, after all, am I not?" he reasoned. Tio C., the leader of the group, said calmly: "Benig, listen to me. I am older than you are. What you are doing is *kagəragtəs* [cursed]. Better drop it while you are not deeply involved yet. Learn from your Tio Maryo. Did he ever make both ends for his family because he maintained an affair with another woman? Remember, marriage is a sacred vow; do not trespass it or your family will suffer." Benig promised to drop the affair. Shamed before the villagers, Sepa left Malitbog hurriedly.

I have not recorded any case of a broken family in Malitbog, in spite of occasional problems like the one cited above. As a rule, a wife is expected to follow what her husband thinks is right for the family. She does not decide on any matter having to do with transactions with other persons, including their immediate kin, without her husband's consent. On the other hand, the husband may do as he pleases, although most of the time he informs the wife about whatever commitments he has made. Work in the field is shared by both husband and wife. During the planting season the husband plows the field, while the wife plants the rice or root crops. Procuring food and other basic needs of the family is the responsibility of the husband, while preparing meals and other household chores are mainly the wife's tasks.

The relations between husband and wife are so commonplace that it is often taken for granted. As some of my male informants said: "After a year of marriage, your wife becomes like a sister to you." The same opinion was expressed by female informants. In matters of public behavior, there is no definite pattern. In going around the barrio, a husband may walk ahead of his wife or he may follow her. Public display of emotions is frowned upon, except in weeping for the dead. Even if a husband has been away from home for a long time, when he returns, the wife will not even give him a "kiss" publicly. The reunion is always casual. The wife often asks the husband how he has been, why it took him so long to come home, and so on. The husband simply turns over to his wife whatever he has brought home with him.

Within the home, however, if no visitors are around, the behavior between the couple changes; but again the display of affection often observable in urban families is absent. When Osing came home from the neighboring town, where he harvested rice, after an absence of six months, he did not even kiss his wife. He fondled and played with the children. During the evening, after a brief huddle with his wife on the balcony of the house, Osing slept in the living room and his wife in another room, with her mother-in-law and the children.

Among the older generation there exists a special type of relationship between husbands and wives, one which is characterized by the inability of either spouse to mention the other's name. This is known as *pahuy,* meaning, calling the spouse's attention by exclaiming *huy!* Tia P., for example, does not directly call Tio C. by his Christian name. I have never heard her do so, even in the most trying situation. If it is absolutely necessary for her to attract Tio C.'s attention, she either goes near him and tells him or sends someone else. Or she makes a sound with her tongue and teeth—psst!—or calls out loudly, *"huy."* Tio C., however, addresses her by her first name.

When I insisted on an explanation of this practice, the reason Rosita gave me for husbands and wives sometimes not calling each other by name is structural.

> You see, before I married him (Insyo), I used to call him *bata?* (uncle). He is my uncle by third cousin. That is, his grandmother and my great grandfather were brother and sister. When we married, I could no longer call him *bata?* because I am his wife. So I resorted to *pahuy.*

This point will be discussed further in Chapter 10.

The relationships between parents and children have already been discussed. Children are expected to respect their parents and to follow what they say. A Malitbog child is better seen than heard. It is considered disrespectful to argue against one's parents; the child is punished for doing so.

When Husi, ten, woke up to find his pet chicken was eaten by the pig, he was very angry. He started beating the animal. The pig scampered around the plaza and Husi chased him around. After a while, his mother called him to stop beating the pig. "It is your fault you did not put your chicken on the roost last night," she said. But Husi did not listen; he continued to beat the pig.

Later, the mother called again. "Will you stop chasing that pig? It will die of exhaustion." Husi, apparently tired and still angry, shouted back: "Eh—why did it eat my chicken? It is better for this pig to die."

An altercation between him and his mother followed. By this time, Amon, the father, returned from the well carrying a bamboo water container. He heard his son answer back the mother. Without saying anything, he went directly to Husi and hit him with a piece of stick, saying: "You should learn better than to answer your mother. You should be ashamed to the neighbors by doing that. They might say I am not teaching you good manners."

Both a mother and a father are responsible for the training of their children. This includes their instruction on proper behavior, such as respect for older people. It is considered disrespectful for a child to mention the name of his parents, either in referring to or taking directly to them. Kinship terms must be used. In speaking to their parents children are expected to lower their voice. Nonobservance of this verbal etiquette means disciplinary action. Thus, when Buding, a 13-year-old daughter of Arsin, answered her mother back when the latter refused to permit her to go to a wake for the dead in the neighboring sitio, she was hit across the mouth by her brother.

The relationship between brothers and sisters is characterized by mutual protection and respect. Older siblings are expected to take care of the younger ones in cases of the parents' death or incapacity due to accident or illness. In turn, the younger siblings are expected to respect their elders and to obey them. Children are constantly reminded about these responsibilities to each other and to their parents by those who are older. The case of Leonardo and his siblings was used by most parents to emphasize this point. When Leonardo's father died, his mother became an invalid. There were seven of them in the family, and he suddenly found himself its head. He was only 12 years old. Neighbors came to help them from time to time, but Leonardo shouldered most of the hard work in keeping the family intact and alive. Early in the morning he would bring the younger siblings to the neighbors' house and them proceed to his work in the field. He would pick them up after he was through with his work. The younger siblings, in turn, respected and obeyed Leonardo as though he was their "parent."

Sibling unity in Malitbog is best exemplified by the cooperative efforts of siblings in sharing the expenses of the marriage of each one of them, in working together in the field during the planting and harvesting seasons, in making or building a house, in sharing food in time of economic crises, and in making important decisions. This deep concern over the welfare of each sibling is almost always carried out through life, although the actual relationship may be characterized by quarrels and other forms of conflict.

Intimacy and friendship characterize the relationship between grandparents and grandchildren. It is known in this barrio that grandparents, as elsewhere in the Philippines, have a tendency to spoil their grandchildren. Misunderstanding generally follows between grandparents and parents when the former intervene in the discipline of the children. Thus when Mal?am Ebi saw Florita beat her child one day, she came to the latter's defense. She scolded her daughter for doing it, saying among other things: "When you were small I did not beat you like that, did I?" Florita did not answer. Continuing, the old woman said: "If you do not like my grandchild, I will bring her home. Why, I can support her. You should be ashamed for what you have done and how you raise your children." Florita and her mother did not talk to each other for a while.

The secrets of growing teen-agers in Malitbog, like adolescent love affairs are shared with grandparents, although they are kept from the parents. "Grandparents are more understanding," informants would say, smiling, "than most parents. They never scold: they advise." Grandchildren can likewise joke with their grandparents, while they cannot (seldom if ever) do so with their parents.

THE HOUSEHOLD

The household is another important unit of Malitbog social organization. It is second to the family in the hierarchy of social groups which surround the child and among whose members he maintains closer contacts and learns the values and practices of the community. As locally conceived, the household is composed of two or more families living in one house; the members share a common kitchen, contribute to the procurement of household necessities (except staple grain) like firewood, salt, and water, prepare and eat their meals separately, exchange cooked food, and sleep in their chosen corners, if the house happens to be a one-room dwelling. Like the nuclear family the household is a consumption unit, with a common protective roof as the unifying factor. What distinguishes it from the nuclear family or the extended family is its size and, in some cases, its membership, which extends beyond the limits of kinship. The extended family has kinship as a point of reference; a household needs not have this framework. A friend or any farm helper of good standing with a family may be taken in as a member of the household until old age, as in the case of Rufo's family, which adopted an old man, Caryas. Caryas was from the mountains and was known to Rufo's family for a long time. When the former's family—composed of his wife and children—was killed by the Japanese soldiers during the war, Rufo took the old man under his roof.

Some close relatives are sometimes taken in, especially unmarried siblings and cousins, because of feelings of love and obligation and the desire to reduce the *pung?aw* (literally meaning, loneliness) of a single kin. As informants said: "To live alone is a very lonely affair." The household oftentimes acts as a single economic unit in which the elementary families work cooperatively with the head of the household, who is usually either the father, the mother, or one of the grandparents. Often, as in the case of Tio C.'s household, it functions merely as a social circle in which the members share the same basic problems, interests, and roof, but remain economically independent of each other.

Thus, Osing, Tio C.'s third son, who lives with him, worries and expresses anxiety over the welfare of his own family and sympathizes with the problems of his married siblings who also live in the same house. He maintains his economic independence, however. One of the major reasons why Tio C. and his wife, Tia P., took their married children under their protective custody is, as Tia P. expresses it, "In lean months, I cannot bear to think of my children and grandchildren getting hungry while I and my husband are having enough to eat." Tio C., incidentally, is employed in the local forestry station. Osing and his brother-in-law are tenants of their father.

In spite of economic independence, the Malitbog household may still be described as a working unit. It is true that work animals are independently owned by the heads of the respective nuclear families, but these can be borrowed by anyone in time of need if the animals are not being used. In the field, the members of the household help each other during planting, harvesting, threshing, and hauling of grains to the house. Most household members farm adjacent fields. During fiestas or other barrio activities—including rites of passage—the entire household contributes its share of responsibility either in kind or labor.

Allocation of authority within the household is based on the ages of its members. Of course the older member (that is, the father or the mother in case of children living with parents) has the final say in all important matters or is consulted by the members before any decision is made. It is the oldest member who represents the household in its relationship with the whole community and intercedes for the members in case they get into trouble. He often acts as guarantor for credit which household members may obtain either from the Government or from moneylenders. The household members may or may not consult each other, each family head planning for his own family independently.

The composition of a Maltibog household does not have a rigidly defined pattern. It changes as new generations of kin are born and as the circle of recognized relatives expands or contracts. The following frame of reference may be taken into consideration relative to the structuring of a household:

1. A newly married couple lives with the girl's parents temporarily for about a year, until the birth of the first child.

2. After the birth of the first child, the couple establish their own independent family, either nearby or away from the family of orientation.

3. Because they have to work in the fields, both parents may take in one or two of their close kin, usually the siblings of either spouse, to stay with the baby while they are away. The kin may stay in the household indefinitely, as long as they are on good terms.

4. Depending upon the economic status of the new family, unmarried first or second cousins or any relative may come to live with the couple—and help in the fields or in the house.

5. The children who marry upon attaining the right age either leave or stay with their in-laws.

Another aspect of Malitbog social organization which lends support to the formation of household units is the absence or rigid rules of residence. As has already been indicated, there is only an initial matrilocal residence, after which a neolocal pattern (that is, anyplace) occurs. Thus there are no restrictions that bar any adult

A young housewife ironing a dress.

member of the family of orientation from staying with the parents even after marriage.

HOUSEHOLD ROUTINE

At day break most of the members of the household, except small children, are awake. The people do not possess clocks or wrist watches, except those who are working the nearby forestry stations. They keep time, however, by watching the movement of the sun and by noting the actions of animals like the cocks, chickens, pigs, and birds. Very early morning is indicated by the rapid crowing of cocks. This is counterchecked by observing the position of heavenly bodies—especially the Southern Cross. When the Cross leans toward the west, the people in the barrio say it is already morning. Time is further indicated by the chirping of the birds and chickens.

Early morning begins with routine activities. Men in their working clothes chop firewood, fetch water from the nearby spring, untie their carabaos from underneath the house or a nearby corral, and start off to work. Women, after enjoying a roll of tobacco or a set of *maramʔən* (rolled betel leaves mixed with tobacco, lime, and areca nut, for chewing), feed the chickens. Grown-up children also prepare for the day's work. The girls gather the laundry and start off for the creek; the boys follow their fathers to the field. Most families do not eat breakfast early, but take it at about eight or nine o'clock, after returning from work.

The people have no fixed schedules of work. Some men stay in the field up to about twelve noon, others, to about ten in the morning. The men plow and first clean the field. Both men and women pick up dried grass and plant the field. The women gather vegetables and prepare meals. Grown-up girls sometimes help pound the rice, although it is normally the men's job. Small children watch the carabaos, the newly planted field, and the *ʔəga* (rice being dried under the heat of the sun). They dig roots for meals.

Mealtime is irregular. Some households eat three times a day, others, only twice. In the case of the latter, breakfast is served about ten or eleven o'clock and supper at about four or five. Cooked rice cakes, or boiled roots of edible plants or bananas are served between meals. Some members of the family eat late, others, early, although the parents normally encourage all to eat together.

After the noon meal both men and women take their naps. Sometimes women pick lice from each other's head. Work in the field starts about three-thirty in the afternoon and lasts up to about five or six. Early evening is characterized by *tubaʔ* drinking by men in the coconut grove, in which women sometimes join. At home the grown-up girls boil sweet potatoes or cassava or cook supper. Eight o'clock is bedtime. A mat is spread on the floor and each one locates himself whereever he wants to lie down. Small children of both sexes sleep together. The grown-up girls sleep inside the *saləd* (small bedroom), if the house has one, or they take the endmost part of the mat, near the wall and separated from the parents by the small children. The boys sleep near the door. Some Malitbog residents do not use mosquito nets; others do.

9 / Circle of close relatives

ASIDE FROM MEMBERS of the family and the household, there is another circle of relatives who are known to and surround the individual. These kin are his playmates in childhood and companions in adult life. From them he learns much about Malitbog culture. They serve as his models for effective social participation. Parents contribute to this learning process by specifying to the children who are their relatives and who are not and what rights and obligations they have among these kin. Proper behavior is likewise emphasized. If the child quarrels with his relatives, he is scolded by the older folks: "Do not fight with your relatives. These are the people from whom you can ask help in time of need. Do you think other people will help you? No—but your relatives will. So be nice to them."

These early prescriptions for acceptable behavior are validated through actual social interactions in adult life. The individual relies mostly on his relatives for assistance in carrying out his numerous social, economic, and religious commitments. In other words, expectations, norms, beliefs, values, and practices which shape juvenile and adult orientation to community life are developed from systems of meaning which are initially learned within the circle of close relatives. This set of conventional rules for behavior functions as the individual's point of reference when interacting with those who are not his kin. It is important then that group perception of kinship be outlined and the norms governing interpersonal relationships among kinsmen be described. If the child understands the lesson of kinship, he can competently move on easily to other types of relations with other people in and outside of the community.

NEAR AND DISTANT RELATIVES

In the course of my fieldwork I noted that in spite of the fact that in Malitbog a wide circle of kinsmen are recognized, reciprocal relations with them are carried out quite selectively. Accordingly, there are relatives whom the individual considers important and others, unimportant, irrespective of whether they are structurally close or distant. Distant kinsmen who become known to him and kin whom he thinks are potentially useful are, moreover, automatically included in the aggregate of close relatives. The actual test of their "usefulness," of course, depends upon the intensity of the kinship relation brought to the fore in later encounters and upon events which lead to such encounters.

There is no local term for this circle of effective, or potentially effective, relatives. Terms like *kadugo?* (blood relations), *kasimaryo* (barriomates), and *linahi* (descent) are sometimes used to refer to this ego-oriented kin unit. When pressed for the term most appropriate to characterize this important kin group, informants failed to offer one. The term which describes the unit closest is *kaparyintihan* (relatives). For lack of a precise Malitbog term for this aggregate of special (that is, potentially useful) kinsmen, I shall use the term "personal kindred," and for the larger circle of relatives, many of whom are not known to ego, the term "kindred."

Not all of the known relatives emerge in group action in time of need. This was the complaint of Mateo when I interviewed him. "When I built this house," he said, "I asked some of my relatives to come and help me. Only three came, out of the ten I asked. See? Also, when I had my child baptized, many of our relatives— that is, my wife's cousins and mine—came only during the feast and partook of the food, but very few came to help in the preparation. Bha—relatives are good only when you have something to offer. If none, other people [nonkin] are much better." I found out later that Mateo himself did not assist those "uncooperative relatives" in the past; hence, they felt justified in not coming when he needed help.

This loose organization of the kindred may be understood in terms of the nature of Malitbog kinship itself. The system is *ego centered*. That is, an individual always considers himself the center of overlapping circles of kin. When situations arise in which two kin or groups of kin are involved, he finds himself in a difficult position. If he takes sides, he loses the support of one set of potentially useful kin; if he remains neutral, he might lose both. As often happens, the individual becomes the mediator in conflicts involving equally related kin. The case which happened in Aming's party in 1964 illustrates this point.

Aming, the brother-in-law of my host, gave a party to celebrate the *pasaka ka ?umagad* (welcoming of the child-in-law). Almost everyone in the barrio came. After several glasses of *tuba?* (coconut wine), Pikto, Aming's second cousin, started to make trouble. Marco, Aming's wife's first cousin, came to talk to Pikto about his "improper behavior in public." However, the latter felt insulted by this act and he boxed Marco on the ear. Marco fell to the floor. When Alfonso, Marco's brother, saw this, he came to his brother's help. The fight became a free-for-all affair, with relatives from both sides joining in. The old men, who were gathered at the backyard, came into the house and broke the fight. As they investigated the cause of the trouble, the relatives of both protagonists again gathered into two groups. Fearing that a yet more bloody encounter would ensue, Aming went into the middle of the room and, in a loud voice, said: "Listen all of you. I did not give this party so you would fight in my house. I gave this because I want all of you to be present, to welcome the newlywed, and to be merry. You should all be ashamed of yourselves. You, Pikto and Marco, are my close relatives. You are my immediate kin and I do not take sides in this case. But I do not want any trouble any more. If you want to enjoy, let us enjoy; if you want trouble, bring it outside—in the open field; not in my house." After this he and other older men approached the protagonists individually and talked to them. The impending bloodshed was averted.

Because of overlapping kindred, as has been pointed out, no two Malitbog individuals, except siblings, have exactly the same number of kin. Each individual considers himself, nevertheless, as the center of a circle of relatives. Depending upon which individual is the point of reference, therefore, each relative assumes a different kinship status in relation to another. As Tonyo, the carpenter, explained it: "My second cousins, for example, may be the fourth cousins of Pedro, who is my third cousin. Not all of my first cousins' first cousins are related to me. That is, their mother's brother's or sister's children are not my relatives. Understand?"

These relationships are further complicated by the high rate of cousin marriages. A cousin marriage is highly preferred for a number of reasons. Cleto outlined some of them, saying, "If you marry your cousin, you are sure she would be [1] loyal to you, [2] obedient to your wishes, [3] understanding of your obligation to your own parents, and [4] concerned about your welfare. Also, you are sure she would not poison you and that she is not an *?aswang* [witch]."

Genealogical survey of the population indicates approximately 60% of the families were established by cousin marriages. Thus, while it is difficult to define with certitude the relationship of each individual in the barrio, the entire community is potentially capable of group action if it is threatened from without. This is exemplified by the manner in which the people bound themselves together when a group of armed men from another town attempted to rob one of the families in the sitio Aglopad in 1964.

The following record of the case appears in my field notebook.

> Early in the morning of May 16, 1964, Consoling and Baldis went to market to sell one of their carabaos. The money was intended for the wedding of their son, Badong, which was scheduled to take place two weeks later. There were a number of men present when the transaction was made.
>
> As the couple prepared to sleep that evening, they heard someone calling for Badong. Baldis stood up to find out who was calling and, as he opened the door, he saw four armed men standing at the foot of the ladder. The bandits told him to keep quiet and to hand over the money to them. Baldis quickly slammed the door and Consoling hysterically shouted for help.
>
> Surprised, the men fired their guns. Baldis and Consoling threw themselves flat on the floor. The gunfire and the voice of Consoling shouting *bandits! bandits!* alarmed the neighborhood. Soon the entire barrio was alive with calls for help and sounds of the *tultug* (a bamboo instrument used to signal for help in case of emergency or to call for a meeting).
>
> Within minutes almost all male members of the barrio were in Baldis' house. However, the bandits were gone. When the men learned about the incident, they grouped together and pursued the bandits, but they failed to catch up with the intruders because it was a very dark night.

RANGE AND DEPTH OF THE PERSONAL KINDRED

A number of factors determine the range and depth of a personal kindred. Among these are: birth, age, residence, degree of mobility, and death. If one is asked about his relationship with a certain person or groups of persons, he replies in terms of a biological connection. "I am the child of ——— [mentions either his mother or father], who is ——— [mentions the relationship] to the relative you mentioned." In other words, the people of Malitbog are aware of the biological structuring of their relationships.

Age is also used as a measure for the structural range of an individual's personal kindred. It should be emphasized that the size of the kindred expands and diminishes as the individual assumes different age-set levels. This was tested by recall. Of course, the effectiveness of recall as a criterion for measuring the number of individuals considered by ego as personal kindred depends upon other factors like spatial mobility, residence, and personality.

At any rate, children informants (age ranging from seven to ten) can recall only their immediate grandparents, granduncles, and aunts in the third ascending generation; parents' and parents' siblings in the first ascending generation, and only the first cousins in their own generation. For the obvious reason of biological age, no kindred is counted from the descending generations.

Between ages 15 and 30 informants are involved in most barrio activities—economic, religious, and social. By this time, many of them have married and have children. The need for assistance in work activities requiring more than one individual brings about the expansion of kindred recognition. Most informants include third, and sometimes fourth, cousins in their effective kinship category.

Residence also contributes immensely to an understanding of the range and character of an individual's personal kindred. Informants who had left the barrio cannot recall as many important relatives as those who stayed. The division of the barrio into sitios adds more weight to the importance of residence as a factor influencing the effectiveness of the personal kindred.

Reinforcing residential membership in defining the range and depth of the personal kindred is spatial mobility. The manner in which individuals locate themselves within or without the barrio affects the nature of their effective ties with their kin. Many families in Malitbog at one time or another moved out of the barrio and returned afterward. Menfolk often leave the barrio for seasonal labor elsewhere, following the agricultural cycle. Two sociological events issue from this seasonal mobility. One is the expansion of one's recalled personal kindred. Working in large farms outside one's own barrio requires the company of relatives or barriomates for security reasons. Most farmers would seldom travel far away in search of seasonal work if they were alone. Normally they go to places where one or two kindred have been or have made previous contacts. Here an individual meets and traces relationship with relatives who were not known to him before and renews and strengthens the one already existing between him and his kinsmen. Thus, the frequency of individual's joining seasonal labor groups influences the structuring of his personal kindred.

FUNCTION OF THE PERSONAL KINDRED

The most important link between relatives is the jural obligation inherent in the relationship. It is expected that all relatives should support each other in group activities and assist the less fortunate members in time of need. This is articulated in the time of crises. Situations which bring it about are frequently associated with social, economic, political, and religious events surrounding each rite of passage in the life cycle of an individual.

A young girl and her brother.

During childbirth, for example, members of the effective kindred come to offer their assistance. Sometimes their help is solicited by either the husband or the wife. Most of those who normally respond are personal kindred of the woman, the reason given by the informants being, "It is our kin whose life is in danger." This statement suggests some kind of loyalty differentiation based on affinal or consanguineal relationship. Basically, the husband's and the wife's personal kindred groups are distantly related to each other.

In time of great need a man first calls upon his own relatives for help, again the reason given by informants being, "You don't lose much face should your request be turned down; after all, they are your kin. But to be rejected by people who are not related to you is more shameful than seems bearable." Thus most affinal relatives are extra careful in their relationship with the husbands or wives of their kinsmen. This is also one reason why women always call for their mothers or mothers' sisters to assist them during delivery.

The above observation seems to indicate that affinal relatives are counted less in time of need. This is not true in actual behavior, even if informants say that they expect less from their affinal kin. In many cases, affinal relatives seldom refuse any request from an affine if only because such rejection will reflect upon the prestige, honor, and pride of the entire personal kindred and not of any specific individual.

Marriage is another factor by which the aggregate of effective personal kindred is mobilized. The average income of Malitbog farmers is never beyond the subsistence level. Statistically, it does not exceed ₱200 (pesos) ($50 U.S. currency) a year. One is surprised, however, that during a marriage an expense amounting to more or less than ₱1000 is met effectively and with apparent ease. The case of Cario, who got married when I was there, illustrates this point. He was the third son in the family of nine. He did not own the carabao which he used to plow the field. The parents were likewise poor. Cario tenanted the land of his third-degree uncle.

One harvest season Cario found himself falling in love with his uncle's daughter, Marit. Cairo and Marit were fourth cousins and this relationship, at least in the barrio, was considered too far off to be tabooed. The expenses from the time Cario sent his parents to ask for Marit's hands to the time they married were as follows:

Pabagti? (preliminary arrangement expenses)	₱ 5.00
Padul?ung (formal arrangement)	180.00
Pangayu? (dowry)	500.00
Kasal (wedding)	400.00
	₱1085.00

In spite of this appalling amount, in terms of local income, Cario was able to get married. His personal kindred came and all of them contributed, in cash and in kind, to the affair.

During economic functions, the most effective kin are those living nearby. As has already been noted, most labor activities are taken free and on a voluntary basis, the *dagyaw*. The same is true in politics. Candidates in the town and province usually count on a wide range of kindred for election to office. Concessions for improvements of the barrio are likewise obtained by the barrio captain from politicians if the latter are assured of kindred votes.

The case of Tio C. illustrates this. When he was barrio captain, a candidate approached him for help. However, he had already promised the votes of his entire family and kin to another. Some people resented this move. The opposing candidate approached Tio C.'s first cousin, who also was a member of a wide kindred group, for support. When Tio C. learned of this, he visited the man and talked to the others. As a concession to him, they gave in and supported Tio C. when he said he would build a schoolhouse of strong materials. This concession, however, did not materialize until after the people saw the materials arrive. Since then, Tio C. has been able to sway the people to his side.

The funeral is another event during the life cycle of an individual in which all his kindred, as well as neighbors, are mobilized for group action. When Badong from Agsiw died in 1964, every member of his kindred—near or remote—came to condole with the family. They also brought their contributions for the funeral and other expenses for the affair.

In carrying out all these rights and obligations to kinsmen, the individual acquires clearer understanding of the beliefs, attitudes, and motives underlying social relations in the community, for the vaguely recalled precepts taught him as a child are now actually experienced in real situations. The prescriptions for roles he has to play cease to be mainly for personal adjustment and satisfaction; they now include preoccupation with what he thinks other people expect him to do and what they think about his performance. The circle of close relatives constitutes the initial group of these "significant other people" with whom the individual carries intimate relations, outside of the family and the household. What he learns from these kin forms the content of his views about the generalized social order.

10 / Wider circle of kin

THE STRUCTURE of a small aggregate of kin, and how it influences local behavior was shown, in the preceding chapter. However, socialization as a process of orienting members of society to the values of group life is not restricted to those activities occurring only within the intimate confines of the family or household. As a man matures, he acquires new statuses and is expected to play new roles. As he becomes more and more involved in nonfamilial affairs of the community, he learns new values and new sets of behavior which are considered appropriate to his position in the group. Although this learning process is not deliberately done or formally organized as in childhood days, it wields, nevertheless, tremendous influence over the direction of adult behavior. For one thing, learning takes place through interactions with people who have influence over what an individual's roles should be and who control rewards and punishments for correct or incorrect actions.

In Malitbog these significant people are mostly kinsmen. Aside from the circle of close relatives there is a host of distantly related kin who also surround the individual and who, although he may not know many of them, expect him to conform to what they hold as appropriate or inappropriate behavior. Deviation from this social requirement has been almost nil in actual situations. The reasons for this are many. The most important one, however, is the view that whatever a person does reflects the honor and prestige of the kin group. If he achieves something, his kinsmen are also praised for it. If he transgresses social norms, they are likewise condemned with him. In other words, kin group expectations often prevail upon the individual to fit his behavior to the demands of the current social norms or he is censured for his deviancy.

This brings us to the importance of kinship in establishing the initial blueprint for the generalized social order in the barrio. By the term "kinship" is meant the system of reckoning relationships among members of the group either by blood (consanguineal), by affinity (in-law), or by *compadrazgo* (ritual). Through these recognized relations are established specific statuses and rules which regulate much of local behavior. Thus a knowledge of the structure of this system is helpful in understanding the situations within which most adult socialization in Malitbog occur.

It must not be construed, however, that the people in the barrio are always thinking about kinship or that they always go about their daily chores with the thought of kinship looming large overhead. Actually, no one talks about kinship unless he is asked to explain about a particular relationship, but even if kinship is not actually talked about, it is socially and culturally recognized. For example, the people clearly distinguish their relatives from those who are not relatives, and thereby adjust their behavior. It is common knowledge among them too that the degree to which an individual is related to another and how—consanguineal, affinal, or ritual—influences the nature of interactions obtaining or expected to obtain between them. In this way, kinship may be viewed as a socialization device through which the average Malitbog farmer develops his definition of situations to guide his actions.

GENERAL CHARACTERISTICS

Malitbog kinship belongs to the bilateral type. This means that an individual reckons relationship equally from both the father's and the mother's sides, whether the linking kin is the father or the mother. The terms "father" and "mother" refer to either the biological progenitors or to the sociological guardians, as in adoption.

There are two ways of looking at Malitbog kinship structure: vertically and horizontally. The vertical structure includes all kin in the ascending and descending generations, with ego as the point of departure. An average man reckons relationship with living or dead descendants up to the third generation and recognizes about five generations in the descending order. The latter group of kin includes his children and four different categories of grandchildren.

The horizontal structure of Malitbog kinship spreads out bilaterally, from ego, and includes first, second, and third cousins (sometimes fourth cousins) from both the father's and the mother's sides. One's own generation is the point of reference in reckoning relationship. The numerical designation of relationship with kin is arbitrary because it can become wider or narrower, depending upon the range of relationship an individual can establish with the members of the generations above him, In a word, the ascending generations are significant in defining the relationships of bilateral relatives within ego's generation. In all cases, however, there is no distinction made between parallel and cross cousins as in unilineal societies. Moreover, any change which occurs in recalling relationships in the upper generation precipitates changes in the tracing of relationship with collateral kin.

TERMINOLOGICAL STRUCTURE

The positions each person occupies relative to each other person in this kinship system are defined in terms they use to call each other. Kinship terms may be described as indicators of social relations between persons in that each term symbolizes certain conventional usages which guide the performance of normative behavior. For example, when two persons call each other "husband" and "wife" or "uncle" and "nephew," reciprocally, they are in effect performing actions indicating that they have certain specific reciprocal rights and obligations to each other.

From this standpoint, kinship functions as a coherent system of social relations expressed in the context of genealogical, affinal, and ritual connections. The key to understanding this system is the terminology speakers use in their dyadic and group interactions.

Malitbog kinship is hard to define in terms of one specific kinship type. On the one hand, it exhibits descriptive characteristics in that *referentially,* the terms *tatay* (father) and *nanay* (mother) are not used to refer to mother's or father's siblings, who are known to ego as *bata?* (parents' male siblings) and *dada?* (parents' female siblings). On the other hand, it also shows classificatory characteristics. The terms for parents are also used to *address* directly the siblings of the parents. The modification introduced is merely the shortening of the kinship terms and the addition of the parents' siblings' personal names after each term. Thus parents' male siblings are *tay* plus the personal name (as in *Tay* Juan), while their female siblings are *nay* plus the personal name (as in *Nay* Petra).

This classificatory principle is even apparent in the grandparental generation. Here, the term applied to the grandparents is also used for their siblings. In fact, relative age and sex of the referants are ignored. Grandparents are known as *?ulang,* and all grandparental kin are classified under one category—the *kamal? aman* (elders).

Within ego's generation, the situation is similar. From the manner in which cross and parallel cousins[1] are grouped together, Malitbog kinship terminology is similar to what anthropologists call the Hawaiian type in that these two sets of cousins are called by the same term as siblings. Elder male sibling is *manung* and elder female sibling is *manang.* Younger siblings are called by their personal names. The only modifications with regard to the use of elder sibling terms are the shortening of the kinship terms and the addition of personal names after the term. However, from the manner in which cross cousins are equated with parallel cousins at the same time that they are separated from siblings by the use of personal names after the kinship terms, Malitbog kinship terminology resembles what is known as the Eskimo type. It is perhaps this characteristic feature which makes Malitbog kinship more flexible in application.

Kinship established by marriage is called *tapik* (attached). The term for husband is *bana* and for wife, *?asawa;* for both referentially, *mag?* asawa. Husbands and wives normally call each other by their first names, unless nicknames are used. When generational positions between husband and wife differ, the wife rarely mentions the name of her husband. Some informants say that they find themselves "embarrassed and would rather refrain from calling the husband's name." The underlying reason for this behavior was explained by one informant:

> I have been so used to calling him (her husband) *bata?* (male uncle from the parental generation) and now he is my husband. I can no longer call him *bata?* and I feel embarrassed each time I have to call him by his personal name. So I decided not to mention the name at all and had stopped calling him *bata?* too.

The term for ego's husband's or wife's male siblings is *bayaw* and for the spouse's female siblings, it is *hipag. Biras* is the term applied to the husband and wife of ego's wife or husband's sister or brother, referentially and vocatively.

Another characteristic feature of Malitbog social organization is the establishment of kinship through the performance of religiously accepted rituals. The term for

---

[1] Cross cousins are children of mother's brother and father's sister, and parallel cousins are children of mother's sister and father's brother.

ritual kinship is *kumpari* (Sp. *Compadre*). This bond is formalized between nonkin when either of the principal actors stand as sponsor for the marriage, baptism, or confirmation of the other's children. Relatives also reinforce their kinship through *compadrazgo.* Although initiated mainly on a spiritual relationship, the tie "actually develops and emphasizes a primary social bond between the parents of children and the godparents; hence, the *compadre* system is best defined as 'ritual co-parenthood' " (Fox 1956:413). Established with this bond, too, are certain rights and obligations between the godparents and the godchildren; the godparents and parents of the godchildren; and between the godchildren and their godsiblings.

The ritual co-parents are expected to help each other in time of need. The god-parents, who are called *maninuy* (male) and *maninay* (female), contribute to the upbringing and education of the child and, reciprocally, the godchild helps in what-ever activities the godparents want done or in resolving whatever difficulties they encounter. The force of these reciprocal rights and duties is as binding as those ob-taining between parents and child. The godparents' advice and sometimes their con-sent is sought before the godchild takes action on major decisions, such as getting married, mortgaging family properties, or applying for loans. In turn, the godpar-ents are expected to provide their godchild with wedding clothes when he gets mar-ried or else underwrite part of the expenses of the wedding feast. The godchild is categorized with the godparents' children and he maintains a quasi-sibling relation-ship with them. They call each other *ʔigsuʔun* and are expected to help one another. While these expectations are ideally upheld, infractions of them have occurred in real situations.

Ritual co-parents call each other *mari* (female) and *pari* (male). These forms of address, as well as the existing relationship are extended to include the siblings of either of the co-parents. The *ʔigsuʔun* relationship, as well as the form of address, is also extended to the children of the godparents' siblings. As among the real siblings, the *ʔigsuʔun* are expected to help each other in times of crises and regard each other as close relatives in the conduct of day-to-day affairs in the barrio. In other words, the network of relationship obtaining through the *compadre-maninuy-ʔigsuʔun* complex is in consonance with the bilateral kinship structure in the barrio, which emphasizes the generational extensional extension of kinship.

KINSHIP AND SOCIALIZATION

As just described, Malitbog kinship functions as an important guide for social behavior in the community. It provides the people with a uniform and specific frame of references for their actions. Through recognized relationships, as indicated by kinship terminologies, they know what behaviors are appropriate or inappropri-ate for what kind of interactions; what social etiquette is necessary and what to dis-regard in interacting with whom; and so on. As Tio C. frequently reminded his grandchildren: "In passing between two older people talking, ask their permission before you pass; show signs of respect by bowing your head a little and by walking slowly. In speaking to those who are older than you are lower the tone of your voice. Remember that all the time."

Since relationship with kinsmen is reckoned bilaterally, an individual is encircled by no less than 200 relatives, coming from both the mother's and the father's sides. These are the people with whom he must get along because they are the ones he can rely on in time of need. Activities carried out within this context, therefore, have consequences for socialization. If he makes good in his work, his kin are there to praise him; if he does something wrong, they are also there to censure him. When Mal?am Ebi expressed this consensus: she scolded her grandson for resenting what Tio C., a distant relative, said about his behavior, "Of course you have no right to resent what you Tio C. has said about your improper behavior at the party. Who else will remind you about your faults? Who else will teach you good manners? Who else will be concerned about your welfare? Your relatives. Your Tio C. is your relative. As an older kin he has all the rights to censure you. Don't be foolish; act like the grown-up that you are."

Reinforcing this bilateral structure of kinship in ordering relationships among the people are two other operational principles: generation and seniority. By "generation" is meant the organizational pattern inherent in the kinship system which sets the members of the group apart from each other in accordance with the order of descent. Thus, members of the parental and grandparental generations are clearly distinguished from the rest of the kin group. Ego's generation consists of siblings and cousins, extending as far as third and fourth cousins. Children and grandchildren are similarly differentiated from each group of relatives.

The relationships between members of these different generations follow certain prescribed rules of behavior. Members of the upper generations are expected, for example, to take good care of their children and grandchildren, in return for which children and grandchildren are expected to obey their parents and grandparents. Infractions of this norm are censured. Thus, when Adis refused to plow for his grandfather when the old man asked him, Tikyo, his father, came that night and upbraided him for his acts. "You should be ashamed for turning your grandfather down," the father said. Adis replied, "But I had already pledged Tuesday for Merto. I agreed to plow for him. How can I work for two people at the same time?" However, the father was insistent: "To whom are you loyal? Merto or your grandfather? Remember he is an old man, your own blood. Who took care of you when you were small? Your grandfather. Now you have the nerve to disobey him. Plow for him on Tuesday. And be sure you come." Tikyo said firmly as he left.

When he was gone, Adis went to Merto and explained to him the situation. Merto did not insist on the previous understanding and everything was resolved. Adis plowed for his grandfather.

This emphasis on generation is reinforced by the concept of seniority. Seniority often transcends biological age. It is actually the sociological point of reference through which the assemblages of kindred are recognized as older or younger members. Through this guideline an individual acquires his status in the group and defines his rights and obligations, reciprocally, with his relatives. Thus even if he were older by five years, Carlos, 50, addressed Juanito, 45, as *bata*? (uncle). On many occasions, I witnessed Juanito order Carlos to do things for him. The latter followed without any complaint. When I discussed this case with him, Carlos explained: "You see, he is my uncle. And even if I am older I am still expected to follow what he says. Actually he is older than I am. His father was my grandmother's brother. You are puzzled, eh? But that is how things are with us here in Malitbog. That is our *surundun* [custom]."

Viewed in this way, it can be seen that seniority and generation are an affirmation of authority and superordination of elders and, equally, of subordination of the younger members. Where doubts about the relationship exist, a kinship term meaning father/mother or older sister/older brother is used; correction is made when the actual kinship relation is discovered.

The clusters of attitudes centering around generation and seniority are best exemplified in the expression of respect and familiarity. These codes of conduct are based on an individual's membership in significant groupings of relatives. Respect, locally known as *taha?*, is an important element in most social situations in Malitbog. An individual who is in disagreement with older members of the barrio seldom shows such feelings verbally, unless necessary. Normally, he may sulk or nod in assent; any verbal clash with an older person or persons, especially in public, is a show of disrespect. Although this ideal norm is generally recognized, actual behavior often contradicts it.

Familiarity or *kilala,* however, characterizes the relationship between persons of equal status, as between siblings and members of the same generations. This is reciprocal only insofar as the referents are within one generation, but not so when they are from different generations. Those in generations below, even if they are close relatives, show respect to those who are above. Most interactions are likewise accompanied by specific gestures, tone of voice, and terms of address indicating familiarity or respect. Rough joking, usually in the form of teasing, characterizes the relations of persons having similar status or coming from the same generation.

Aside from these specific rules of conduct, kinship in Malitbog forms the basis for the establishment of group alliances. In fact, the boundaries of the community's social universe are often expressed in terms of kinship. This does not in any way suggest that the people are unaware of the political boundaries of the barrio because they well know the extent of its jurisdiction. However, in terms of group identity the boundaries do not coincide with the political-territorial limits. Once an individual is known as *tiga*-Malitbog (that is, from barrio Malitbog), he remains a *tiga*-Malitbog regardless of his future residence. It is not uncommon, therefore, to hear people from the neighboring barrios say of a Malitbog individual: "He is from Malitbog, only he is residing here because he married one of our barriomates." In a similar vein residents would volunteer information about those who came to settle in the barrio: "They are not from this place; they came from another barrio and we are not related to them." Here the place of residence is not only equated with kinship but is defined in that context as well.

In speaking of *tiga*-Malitbog, as seen in the context of kinship, the people are in effect making certain differentiations between their own membership group and those of others. This sense of introspection involves group norms, attitudes, and values which influence a person's appraisal of his own conduct. It is these reference groups which structure the "mental world of the individual, in the sense that they furnish organized perspective and ways of looking at society" (Radcliffe-Brown 1952:49). In short, techniques for social behavior in or outside of the barrio are first learned within the circle of kinsmen.

11 / Social order and value orientation

REINFORCING THE NETWORK of relations within which the people of Malitbog function as members of the society are some culturally established standards of behavior that serve as guides to many social interactions. These standards may be analyzed in terms of two systems of behavior, contingent with local definitions and evaluations of situations involved. One deals primarily with sets of collective responsibilities over certain social behaviors which I call "relational imperatives." The other deals with sets of beliefs that articulate supernaturally prescribed modes of conduct which, for lack of a better term, I call "teleological imperatives." Although these two systems can be conceptually separated and analyzed, they are in actual practice intertwined and bound up with expectations the people have of each other. These established standards are learned in childhood, reinforced or modified in puberty and adolescence, and put to actual practice in adult life; they constitute the fundamental educational mechanisms that mold an individual into an acceptable member of Malitbog society.

RELATIONAL IMPERATIVES

Neighborhood. The concept of "being neighbors" is basic to Malitbog social life. All processes and procedures which regulate behavior involve the aggregate of people one referentially calls *kaʔingod* or *ʔiningod*. Spatially, *kaʔingod* refers to small aggregates of close neighbors, people living in the "next" house while *ʔiningod* refers to a larger group residing "within the environs." This dichotomy has reference to physical proximity of household units in terms of degree of daily interaction. Close neighbors interact more frequently than distant ones and therefore have a more cohesive bond of common interests.

In spite of sentiments that attach members closely to each other, the neighborhood has no autonomous existence in itself. It is not bound by fixed social, legal, traditional, or physical landmarks within the barrio. Its existence, therefore, is wholly dependent upon the intensity of interactions obtaining between its members and of the social content involved in their relationship. Should anyone become disgruntled with his neighbors, he can move to another group and there establish local attachments. On the whole, however, it is in the context of the small neighborhoods within which society operates. For one thing, the neighborhood is deeply rooted to the life sphere of the farmers; for another, it represents the most effective segment of rural society where collective responsibilities of social control are best carried out.

As a social unit, the neighborhood functions primarily in areas of group life which are not served by the immediate nuclear family, the household, nor by the whole community. It may therefore be characterized as a sociological construct—a conceptual frame of reference which, even if it is not verbalized by the people, serves as an outline in defining sets of relationships that are vital to the functioning of the barrio as a whole.

Neighbors are expected to help one another in time of great need or even in ordinary chores which require the assistance of other persons. It is not uncommon, in this respect, to hear someone call for the neighbor to "please watch over our house while we are away." A mother may request a neighbor to keep an eye on her child or children while she goes to market or works in the field. A person delayed by other pressing business in town during market days will usually look for a neighbor and send home through him what he has purchased, a practice known as *ʔulayhon*.

On special occasions neighbors are expected to come and assist in such chores as helping in the kitchen, butchering the livestock, fetching water, gathering feul, and other jobs necessary to make the occasion fitting and successful. On other occasions, they act as intermediaries for marriage arrangements and as retinue of the bridegroom and the bride during the marriage ceremonies. Should a carabao get loose during the night, a neighbor is called to help recover it. The people also unite when necessary against a common enemy, like cattle rustlers, bandits, and other outsiders, by organizing themselves into night patrols known as *runda*.

The trait most expressive of the neighborhood sentiment and of its selective nature is the *garalwanay* or reciprocal exchange of food. Every time a person brings home foodstuff, cooked or uncooked, he sends a plateful or a portion to the neighbor with whom he maintains close ties. Cooked food exchanged for this purpose are: chicken, beef, pork, seafood, *pansit* (noodles), and canned goods. This reciprocal food exchange strengthens the neighborhood relationship. It can also weaken this relationship. By failing to meet his expected obligations, one individual disappoints another and conflict emerges. The former is branded by the latter as *kaʔəm* (stingy), *mahakəg* (greedy), and other terms signifying an unwillingness to share. This means the end of their good relationship.

The significance of neighborhood cooperation, especially in economic pursuits, is best exemplified in the group work known as *sulʔug*, or *dagyaw*. *Sulʔug* is a free and reciprocal service rendered to any member of the barrio in the spirit of neighborliness. It is either solicited or voluntarily given, but whoever initiates the group work imposes upon himself the obligation to return the favor of those who respond to the call.

Apparently, more work is done during a *sulʔug*. The individual who lags behind during a *sulʔug* is likely to be branded as an *ʔuyayaʔ* (a slow foot) by his fellow workers, and this hurts his dignity and social prestige. The joy and fun that usually go with the activity characterize the *sulʔug*. As they work, the men sing, tell stories, relate interesting experiences, discuss problems concerning the welfare of the barrio, and many other things—all of which enliven the activity.

The *kumbuya* is another kind of communal labor in which a group of men or women pool their resources and undertake certain projects with the end in view of profiting from their joint effort. Unlike the *sulʔug*, the *kumbuya* is a formal partnership with profit-sharing, and this group work is generally employed in harvesting rice and corn, in building a house, and in catching freshwater fish.

Huyaʔ Another fundamental concept crucial in understanding recurrent and consistent behavior in the barrio is *huyaʔ*. This term is translated as "self-esteem," *dignidad, amor propio,* and *dəngəg* (honor). Its nearest popular English equivalent is "shame."

Huyaʔ is put into practice when what is infringed upon deals with relationships pertaining to (1) personal dignity or honor of the individual; (2) the status or position of the principal actor relative to other people; (3) the internal cohesion of the family as a unit; and (4) the reputation of the entire kin group relative to the outside world. A violation of speech etiquette—that is, the tone of the voice, the choice of words, and the like—also generates *huyaʔ*. In the latter, the people have a specific term, *saklaw,* which is close to the English "embarrass." *Huyaʔ* is expressed in the attitudes, emotional attachments, and behavior relative to socioeconomic life, religion, morality, and individual decorum.

My first encounter with *huyaʔ* was in 1956. When I arrived in the barrio, it was the end of the planting season. This time of the year is always critical in that food is scarce and the prices of staples are high. Even those economically well off complain of hardships. This is the time of the year when foodstuffs like tubers and roots are not yet ripe and corn is not yet harvestable.

Although I mentioned that I brought my own food supply, my host told me to keep it for the time being. Surreptitiously, his wife sent a small boy to the pastor's house to borrow a canful of white rice. No one joined me while eating; the children were gathered around, hungrily watching me and making occasional guttural swallows. They were told to stay away and they did.

Later, I learned that to have nothing to offer a stranger upon arriving in one's house is *kahuruyaʔ* (shameful). Except when there are visitors, the people would seldom borrow staples from neighbors, unless they are close relatives. Asked why, Tia P. said, "It is good if they will lend you, but if not, you will be shamed. It is like 'selling' [that is, making public] your shortcomings; people will talk."

In other words, everything is done to camouflage one's economic difficulties to other people, especially newcomers. Among themselves, some degree of leveling exists which minimizes the sentiments attached to *huyaʔ*. For example, they know that during certain parts of the year almost everyone is in need. It is, therefore, not so shameful to admit that one has nothing to eat. In the final analysis, this is to one's advantage because it forewarns potential borrowers about the difficulty. Hence, they would not press their attempt to borrow rice.

Generally, to insist on borrowing is humiliating. Under normal circumstances, the people in Malitbog would never insist, but in difficult times, one forgets the norm. As the barrio captain said, "You have to bear the brunt of your shame, otherwise you go hungry." Thus such statements as *waʔay huyaʔ* (without shame) or *patay ʔet huyaʔ* (bereft of shame) are commonly heard from lenders when they fail to collect from borrowers after several attempts. From the borrower's point of view the collector is also *wa?ay huya?* or *patay ?et huya?* in that he keeps coming back, despite their promises to pay. Such attitudes are often the root of quarrels in the barrio. What is most resentful is not that one cannot meet his obligations, but that the creditor's presence shames the debtor before other people.

How one dresses himself in the barrio is closely linked with his anticipations of how other people feel about him. To wear clean clothes every day is to invoke such comments as: "*Daw si sin?o ka gid. Indi? ?ikaw mahuya? magpadayaw.dayaw diyan sa baryu?* [You think as if you are somebody; are you not ashamed of yourself-showing off in the barrio?]. "Correspondingly, a newcomer who immediately dons dirty clothes hoping that he might be accepted by the people as one of them is apt to be regarded as very insulting. Not being part of the group, he is expected to behave differently. To imitate the way the barrio folk dress is a breach of proper conduct; the act is often interpreted as adding insult to injury, especially if the newcomer comes from the city.

On certain occasions, however, everyone is expected to don appropriate attire. This means a clean shirt, trousers for males, and clean blouse and skirt for females. To impress her peer group that she had just arrived from the city where she was working, Andoy's daughter put her black jeans and thin blouse to go to the party held in honor of her newly baptized nephew. When her father noticed her attire he immediately upbraided her: "You are shameful. Go home and dress properly. You look humiliating, like an ill repute. Do you like to be the talk of the people here?"

The girl tried to argue her way, but her mother came to her father's defense. Soon every relative was commenting on her attire. While it looked nice on her and while she admitted it was the fashion, still her aunt stated, "It is good if we are the only people, among ourselves. But there are visitors and what will they think? It is indeed *kahuruya?* [shameful]. Go home and change it." The girl relented.

The awareness about *huya?* in relation to dressing is developed early in childhood, when children are impressed with the need for clothes. A five-year-old child who goes around naked is at once scolded and told not to display his genitals: "You are old enough to be ashamed of yourself." This is interesting in that many boys, age ranging from six to seven, run around the barrio without any pants at all. By the time the children have grown up they are fully aware of *huya?* and its implications in terms of one's self-esteem and of one's family position in the community. It needs to be emphasized in this connection that an individual's wrongdoing reflects not only his person but on how the parents have failed in his education.

The common expression *mahuya? ta* (we will be shamed) clearly shows this pattern of expectations. Thus when her little boy brought home the toy dog of the neighbor, Clarit was very mad. She scolded the child: "Go—return that toy or I will peal your buttocks with a piece of stick. What will people in the neighborhood think—I am not teaching you good manners?" The boy ran and returned the plaything.

Clarit's deep concern over what her little boy did exemplifies the degree to which internalization of the norm takes place. The behavior of the child is considered a reflection of the family's standing in the community—that is, they are good or bad, depending upon how well behaved the members are. It is the same in the world of the adults. Whatever an individual does also involves the reputation of the family.

Reciprocity   Closely associated with *huya?* are two other fundamental norms that underlie Malitbog dyadic and group behavior. These are *?utang nga kabaraslan* and *?utang nga kabubut?on*. They form the basic framework of reciprocity in the barrio. As a system of social usage, *?utang nga kabaraslan* and *?utang nga kabubut-?on* is approximated by any of these English phrases: debt of goodwill, debt of gratitude, or debt of generosity of the heart; while *?utang nga kabaraslan* means debt to be repaid, reciprocated, or vindicated.

These two categories of social debts are functionally differentiated by the manner in which they are incurred. *?utang nga kabubut?on* is established through unsolicited, voluntary extension of assistance in the form of gifts or services to someone else, while *?utang nga kabaraslan* is created through solicitation of another person's help or services in realizing the goals desired. Once initiated, the contractants of the reciprocal obligations expect to receive from each other services, gifts, or assistance of equal value or kind. The degree of involvement in the consequent social interaction is proportional to the length of the relationship and the status of persons concerned.

If the *kabaraslan* is carried out with friends, relatives, and neighbors, the psychological commitment is of shorter duration. As soon as repayment in kind or services has been made, the relationship ceases to be defined in the context of reciprocity. None of the participants feel the qualms of obligations, and the underlying feeling of *huya?* they have to each other does not come to the fore in the face-to-face interaction. This is best exemplified in communal work in agriculture, in building or transferring a house, and in other odd jobs.

If the principal actors come from different socioeconomic statuses, the sense of obligation involved in *kabaraslan* is of longer duration on the part of the initiator, while it may be minimal on the part of the respondent. The vertical nature of the base accounts for this unequal involvement in the value system. For example, when a farmer requests the clerk at the municipal treasurer's office in the town to help him with his papers, he creates an *?utang nga kabaraslan*. The next time he comes to town the farmer brings to the clerk's house eggs, chickens, vegetables, and fruits, but the feeling of obligation is not terminated. The status of the clerk is much higher and the service rendered is beyond the capacity of the farmer to perform. Moreover, the fact that the clerk attended to his request is proof that the clerk is kind hearted. Here, the commitment shifts somewhat from pure *kabaraslan* to *kabubut?on*. Thus even if the title of his land and other papers pertaining to it were accomplished five years ago, Baldis would still remember his relationship with the clerk in town. He would shake his head and say, "You see, my debt of obligation to [name the clerk] is indeed big. I can't possibly repay him. For without his help, my papers would have not been in order up to this time. He is really a good man."

?utang nga kabubut?on does not operate within the nuclear family. It is *?utang nga kabaraslan* which is weighted as the reinforcing principle in interfamilial relationships. As I see it, this is perhaps due to the fact that inherent in the structural relationships of individuals in the family are specific rights and obligations. These rights and obligations are kinship defined, making the relationship a required one.

That is, it is the right of the children to demand support and protection from the parents, and it is the parents' obligation to provide these in return for their right to demand obedience and respect.

Outside of the family, however, as well as within the narrow confines of close relatives, the *?utang nga kabaraslan* is pervasive. The boundaries of these two concepts of social obligations are largely determined by the kind of relationship the contractants have, the propinquity of residence, the frequency of interactions, and the level of socioeconomic status in the community.

OTHER FORMS OF LOCAL ETHICS

Among the other most frequently mentioned concepts through which the farmers in Malitbog express their feelings and pass their judgments are: *patugsiling, kabalaka, kalolo?, kakugi?,* and *kapisan.* These may be described as the "cardinal virtues" of the people. The nearest English equivalent of *patugsiling* is compassion. It connotes the ability to subordinate one's own interest in favor of someone else. Should an individual show an unreasonably domineering attitude over someone else, the farmers would frown and say, "Don't you have any *patugsiling?*" or "Have *patugsiling* over him, you might be in the same boat tomorrow."

Kabalaka refers to an individual's deep concern over somebody else's welfare or over a task undertaken. It connotes unselfish consideration of another person's well-being. Parents will usually tell their elder children to have *kabalaka* over the welfare of the younger siblings. Likewise, both husband and wife are enjoined during marriage to have *kabalaka* over each other's health, feelings, and tasks in supporting the family and in bringing up the children.

Kalolo? refers to tenderness of the heart. It encompasses the individual's ability to feel another's inner emotional needs. It could also mean love, kindness, sympathy, unselfishness. A sibling is said to have *kalolo?* if he is considerate, loving, and is concerned over the welfare of his siblings as though it were his own. He has *patugsiling* too. The latter is much deeper, and *kalolo?*, while as deep, is easily perceived. Between husband and wife, the *kalolo?* concept is perceivable if the husband takes care of the wife's needs, understands her likes and dislikes, and tries by every means to please her. A corresponding treatment is expected of the wife. As an ideal norm, the *kalolo?* relationship is a goal every Malitbog man and woman dreams of and strives to attain. Anyone falling short of this ideal is branded as *wa?ay ?et kalolo?* (without tenderness) or *wa?at patugsiling* (without compassion).

Kakugi? and *kapisan* have reference to industry and hard work. A man who attends diligently to his work is known as *mapisan* and his attention on details and thoroughness in every endeavor is known as *kakugi?*. These two ideal norms also constitute the criteria on which Malitbog parents base their judgment in selecting spouses for their children. A *mapisan* boy would likely be the much sought after male in the barrio; similarly, a hard-working girl is the object of every man's heart.

TELEOLOGICAL[2] IMPERATIVES

A number of traditional beliefs which underlie local behavior and reinforce the basic secular ethics of the community exist in the barrio. Of these, *gaba*?, *?ulin*, *?abay*, *tukdo*, *tuyaw*, and *langdayan* are of great importance.

The *gaba*? literally means "curse" or punishment received from the supernatural beings or from God for doing things contrary to the accepted norms of the barrio. For example, a man who lays a hand on an older person will surely suffer from the *gaba*?. The punishment may not be meted out right away, but, as one of my informants said, "Who can escape the wrath of God?" The words of the parents are generally accepted as the words of God and whoever disobeys his parents suffers the *gaba*? which God has hallowed parental authority. Ridiculing other persons because of some physical deformity will be enough to cause the *gaba*?. One will receive the *gaba*? not only by insulting older people but also by not respecting the grace of God. For example, if an individual wastes his rice, the rice will curse him and he will suffer misfortunes. The *gaba*? can be obviated only when a man repents what he has done.

Similar to the *gaba*? is another traditional belief called *?ulin*. This is based on the assumption that an individual will eventually suffer the same degree of humiliation he caused the offended person. Those who laugh at someone else's deformity, for example, will have the same deformity, or one of his children will have it.

> Susing, Jose's sister-in-law, visited a friend one day. The latter had just given birth to an infant which had a split upper lip, locally known as *sungi*?. Susing could not help but smile in amusement. When her own baby was born, it was also *sungi*?. People say *"na ?ulinan"* (she was cursed).

The object of ridicule determines the type of suffering to be borne by the one ridiculing. If one laughs at a defect in another man's carabao, his own carabao will have the same defect.

The *?abay* is an inborn power which causes others misfortunes. For example, if one is in the company of an *?abayən*, he will always have difficult times obtaining what he wants. A menstruating woman is said to be *?abayən;* so is a pregnant one. "Should they pass by you while you are fishing, you will not catch a fish," said Aming when I asked him to explain why an *?abayən* is not brought to help in such endeavors as fishing. Ripening vegetable gardens or rice fields are not accessible to women having their monthly menstruation or to those who are pregnant, as it is believed that the fruit and flowers of the plants will fall.

The *tuyaw* is a supernatural punishment inflicted on those who ridicule the rituals or laugh at the practices of the medium or the herb-medicine practitioner. People will say "you are *natuyawan*," meaning the supernatural being is angry at you. This concept is related to *langdayan*. The latter is specific. If a person

---

[2] As stated previously, the term teleological is used advisedly and with reference to the local belief that human destiny is partly determined by an over-all design in the universe, mediated through the supernatural powers. Any infringement of the prescribed traditional beliefs, therefore, causes human sufferings.

ridicules the works of the medium, he will die or will lose his mind. Here is a case.

> Consoling was a teacher. During her first day in Malitbog there was a *baylan* (medium) ceremony. It was a major one, offered to the sick persons. Consoling and her friends attended the ritual dance. When they returned home that night, they laughed and mimicked the dance. A few weeks later, Consoling lost her mind. She started laughing and crying and dancing. The people said she was *na langdayan* or cursed for laughing at the sacred work of the medium.

Opposite to the *gaba*ʔ is a more positive means of social control, the *grasya* or grace of God. It is received either from God or from the supernatural beings which abound in the Malitbog natural environment. In early life this idea is impressed upon a child by the parents through stories and other examples. Rice, corn, and other foodstuff are taken to be *grasya* of heaven. Therefore, whoever throws away or wastes foodstuffs will surely suffer from *gaba*ʔ. The food will "feel bad and run away from the erring individuals," hence the individuals will suffer from misfortunes.

Tukdo mean revenge. It is a form of *balǝs* (to return or reciprocate). The people in Malitbog maintain this sentiment. They call it *tukdo*. Other related terms are ʔ*unung, dǝmǝt,* and *himalǝs.* The nearest English equivalent of these is revenge, a vendetta. Any person whose kindred or parents have been insulted, beaten up, or killed has the right to *tukdo*. He usually seeks revenge when someone hurts a loved one. The sentiment of *tukdo* is taught early in childhood and re-emphasized in adult life. The following case illustrates the functional reality of this concept.

> Malʔam Intes had a son, Romeo. Romeo was attending school in a neighboring barrio. One day Romeo was boxed by another boy. He went home and told his father about the unprovoked fight. When the boy passed by the barrio, Romeo's father beat him. The boy ran home, and soon his family and kindred came (*surung*) to attack Romeo's father. They also demanded an explanation. Until the case was settled in the mayor's office in town, there was a series of fist fights between Romeo's family and kindred and the kinsmen and family of the other boy.

12 / The supernatural world

ONE OF THE UNDERLYING PRINCIPLES in child training and adult orientation to the norms of Malitbog society is the development of individuals who are easily controlled. This includes making an individual aware of the circle of kin which surrounds him and of his relation to every kindred. There are rules governing social and moral activities in the barrio that reinforce kinship ties. These rules are anchored to a set of beliefs concerning the existence of supernatural beings. These nonhumans, who inhabit the surrounding world, participate actively in the daily affairs of man. They cause illness and misfortune to those who do not observe the rules of conduct; they reward those who are obedient and faithful. Thus the people of Malitbog must square accounts with the spirits by observing the conventional norms of behavior if they are to live in security and peace in the barrio. Malitbog society is viewed as a small part of a wider natural-social universe inhabited partly by spirits and partly by humans. The social prescription for so many human actions is felt to come from metaphysical demands. The pattern of social life is fixed because it is part of the general order of the universe, and even if this were hardly understood and regarded as mysterious, it is nevertheless accepted as invariant and regular.

STRUCTURE OF THE UNIVERSE

The universe is conceived as divided into three major parts: the ʔudtohan (upperworld), the katungʔanan (middleworld), and ʔidadalman (underworld). Each of these parts or worlds is peopled by supernatural beings, known generally as the ʔengkanto. They are thought to possess powers and authority over certain aspects of human life in that they hold offices which specifically define their relationships with human beings.

The spirits of the upperworld are grouped according to the place where they reside. Those living in the zenith of the sky are known as ʔudtohanan. It is believed that God resides in this place together with some of his favorite angels. They are the most kind and virtuous of all the supernatural beings. God and these few chosen angels are, however, so remote that they are seldom conceived as actively participating in the affairs of man. They wait in this highest world and pass final judgment on everyone.

The residents of the next highest level of the upperworld are known as langitnən.

The term is derived from the word *langit,* meaning the sky. The spirit gods of this region are as gentle as the angels in the *ʔudtohan.* They have few but important contacts with human beings. Those who have direct contacts with man are the ones residing in the *ʔawanʔawan* or the space between the clouds and the sky. These are the spirits who control the wind, the rain, the lightning, the storms, and the typhoons. Saints live in this part of the universe. That is why they can hear the prayers of man.

The second lower layer of Malitbog universe is inhabited by a myriad of spirits known as *dutanʔən.* Tradition states that the *dutanʔən* were originally spirit gods who resided with God in the upperworld. However, when *Lusiper* (Lucifer) revolted against the wishes of God, the Almighty threw him and his followers out of *ʔudtohan.* Those who fell into the bowers of the trees became the *tumawo* (fairies); those who fell in deep forest became the *talunanən;* those who fell in rivers and streams became the *tubignən;* and those who fell into the sea became the *tabuknən.* The places where these supernatural beings live are tabooed, much feared grounds known as *palhi.*

The third and lowest level of the universe is located deep in the bowels of the earth. The earth is conceived as a piece of big dried mud, supported underneath by a stone framework, which is hollow inside. Inside the hollow live the *maligno,* the spirits of the underworld. Entrance into this place is through a *bungalog.* The *maligno* are malevolent spirits. They keep pets like snakes, lizards, crocodiles, and many other animals. Pestilence, diseases, agricultural pests, and other forms of bad luck in life are attributed to the doings of the *maligno.*

CONTACTS WITH THE SUPERNATURAL

Contacts with the supernatural beings are made through visits to or unintentional trespass of sacred grounds, attendance in special seances performed by the mediums, and through ordinary encounters. Most encounters take place in tabooed grounds which include parts of cliffs, boulders, caves, springs, thickets, solitary bamboo groves, deep pools, underground tunnels, and headwaters of streams and rivers. Thus, lingering near or roaming around these places is considered dangerous. The spirits do not want intruders into their home grounds, and those who trespass this prohibition, intentionally or unintentionally, are dealt with accordingly.

The fear of contact with supernatural beings is brought about by the consequence which follows the encounter. Illness is said to result from all contacts. The ailments may take the form of severe headache, stomachache, fever, loss of mind, and even death. The most dangerous of all the preternaturals is the *ʔaswang* because they are believed to "eat human flesh and internal organs, especially the liver." Most of my informants who said they had been attacked by an *ʔaswang* refused to go out alone at night. No one can defeat the *ʔaswang*'s powers because of his anti-*ʔaswang* charms.

Reports of contacts with supernatural beings are many and varied. These may be divided into two major categories: sensory and visual. The former includes olfactory, auditory, and tactile contacts; the latter includes visual imagery and actual physical encounters.

SENSORY

Olfactory phenomenon This phenomenon involves the sense of smell. Informants testify that the scent they often smell is either sweet or offensive, depending upon the occasion and place of the experience. If an individual happens to be near the *bubug* (a tree with a big bower), he has more chances of smelling the odor of cooked food. Fried onions and garlic are the most frequently smelled food; the smell of newly harvested upland rice, as well as those used for rituals, ranks next. Should an individual happen to be near tabooed springs and headwaters, especially at noon, he is likely to smell the refreshing scent of toilet soap, as though someone is taking a bath nearby. Here is a case.

> Marcelo, a 25-year-old son of Tara, one of the village elders, was plowing his field. Toward noon he stopped working, drove his carabao to graze, and he himself sought the headwaters of Malitbog creek. The place was described as *mari?it* [tabooed]. As he approached the spring, he smelled the scent of toilet soap, as though someone was taking a bath. He thought it was his sister. So he kept walking and when he was near the spring he saw a beautiful woman. She was fair in complexion, with long hair and a shapely bosom. Marcelo could not remember having seen any woman in the barrio like her. A thought dawned on him: may be she was one of the American missionaries who came to help in the local Protestant church.
>
> Marcelo gave a cough to warn the woman of his presence. The woman turned her back and Marcelo lowered his eyes to avoid hers. It was a matter of seconds and when the young man looked up the woman was gone. Frightened, he ran home. Everybody agreed that the woman he saw was a *tumawo*. Many volunteered having smelled the same odor, especially during noontime.

Familiar odors may be smelled when an individual is alone or when he is with a companion, although the latter may not experience the sensation.

> One day I was walking with one of my informants across the barrio. Suddenly, he stopped and looked up toward the nearby tree and said, "They must be preparing lunch."
>
> "Who are?" I asked.
>
> "The dwellers of the trees," he said as we continued walking.
>
> "How did you know?"
>
> "Did you not smell fried onions?" he said. I answered I smelled nothing.
>
> Shrugging his shoulders he said: "Well, wait until they know you—then you will see them; they will reveal themselves."

The spirits are believed to be *malihi,* meaning strict observers of specific taboos. They do not reveal themselves to anybody, nor do they make their lifeways known to strangers because if they do, they will die. That is the reason why newcomers in Malitbog cannot smell, hear, or see the doings of the environmental spirits.

Auditory phenomenon Hearing voices is another phenomenon which is frequently noted by the farmers. It can take place when one is alone in the open field, near lonely bamboo groves, or even inside the house. Auditory experiences are classified as follows: *bahoy, marukpuk, pangaruskus, mirispis, wakwak, tiktik,* and *wilik.* Human voices, calling for someone when approaching the house, are also heard.

The *bahoy* is characterized by voices of weeping and groaning human beings. The phenomenon is always associated with death, either due to an accident, or murder, or drowning. Many places in Malitbog are thus identified as sites where one would likely hear the *bahoy,* especially during noontime. These are places where Japanese soldiers and Filipino guerrillas were killed during the last war.

The *murupuk* is heard in bamboo groves. It is characterized by sounds of breaking bamboo trees as though someone is cutting them; rattling of twigs and leaves as though a strong wind, even if the atmosphere is calm, is tearing them; and of beating of bamboo stems as though someone is playing with a piece of stick. Most *murukpuk* sounds are heard during noontime or midafternoon, usually around 3:00 P.M. Informants explained that the *marukpuk* are spirits of the dead which haunt bamboo groves where poles used to carry the coffins to the cemetery have been cut.

Another auditory phenomenon which is reported frequently, but only at night, is the *panguruskus,* characterized by scratching sounds against the walls, as though by clawed creatures which no one has ever seen. The people who have heard the sound, however, say that this "is the sign that the ?*aswang* is near the house." ?*ugtak* is the sound associated with the *bawa,* pets of the supernatural beings. The *bawa* like to play in stoves and to eat live embers. The ?*ugtak* is described as similar to the clucking of the hen. Every now and then my host would call my attention to the clucking of the *bawa,* but I never heard it.

The return of the spirits of the dead and the coming of an impending danger is announced by the chirping of the *mirispis.* The *mirispis* is described as a small, blackish, cricket like creature. It gives deep, sharp, eerie chirps. If the creature perches on rooftops and gives the sound, the ghost is said to be coming; if it chirps near the door, someone in the family will soon die; if near the window, an impending danger is in the vicinity.

Informants likewise report hearing calls from someone approaching the house. When they look out to see, no one is there. Here is a case.

> One day, toward noon, Aming and his wife visited Rufo and his family. Rufo's elder son was ill. While they were talking and chewing betel, someone called out from the yard. It was the voice of Tia P., wife of Tio C. Aming, who was seated near the door, leaned further out and said, "Come in. We are just talking about you."
> Everyone waited. No one came in. Clarit, Rufo's wife, stood up and looked out of the window. "There is no one downstairs." This alarmed everybody. So they called out to Tia P. who lives across the plaza. She vehemently denied having left the house. Everyone agreed it was the *tumawo.*

Tactile phenomenon   Another preternatural experience which Malitbog farmers report expression of fear and abomination is tactile in nature. That is, a person reports being visited by an apparition during the night and experiencing being touched by it. The touch is described as cold and "lifeless." It is coupled with olfactory experience involving smelling of burnt incense and candles. Sometimes these phenomena occur in the form of a cold waft of breeze passing an individual's face or the nape of his neck. Other sensory phenomena combine with tactile ones in making the individual shiver with fright. Illness usually follows tactile experiences.

VISUAL EXPERIENCES

As in sensory phenomena, visual experiences include seeing the *bagat,* the *sarut,* the *santirmu, mantiyu, kama²kama², sigbin,* and the *²aswang.*

The *bagat* are seen only during the night, especially when there is a full moon, or when the night is extremely dark and when there is a drizzle earlier in the evening. The *bagat* are normally harmless, although they can be dangerous when harmed. They appear in the form of cats, dogs, pigs, horses, carabaos, birds, and so on. Some people associate the *bagat* with the *²aswang;* others separate them, saying that the *²aswang* may take the form of the *bagat,* but there are also *bagat* which are pets of the supernatural beings. There are specific areas in Malitbog where people frequently see the *bagat.* Such places are known as *bagatan.*

Closely related with the *bagat* are the *sarut.* These take the form of queer-looking animals and insects which situate themselves in places where humans might be tempted to harm them. When left alone, the *sarut* are harmless, but when unduly hurt, they retaliate by making the offender sick. The *sarut* could be aptly described as the supernatural tempter.

When the evening is characterized by showers and thunderstorms, most Malitbog adults prefer to be inside the house. Walking around the barrio predisposes one to encounter the *santirmu,* usually in the form of a ball of fire, although sometimes it appears in the form of burning hillside or corn field. The *santirmu* is associated with murder or with raw, unnatural death known as *hilaw nga kamatayon.*

The *kapri* is a dark, tall man with a hairy body. He resides in big, abandoned houses. Many Malitbog farmers say they had seen a *kapri* visit the barrio, but they do not believe these nonhumans reside in the village. Like other supernatural beings, the *kapri* also behave like humans, and they drink, gamble, and smoke. Juan, a neighbor, tells that one morning he was grazing his carabao near the corn field. Because it was cold, he pulled a roll of tobacco from his pocket and struck a match to light it. Suddenly he heard a voice behind him saying, "Can I have a light?" Juan looked up and he saw a big man. Shaken by fright, he was speechless; he merely handed his match to the stranger. The *kapri* lighted his tobacco, returned the match, and walked away. Juan was unconscious when he was found by another farmer.

Another huge humanlike supernatural being is the *mantiyu.* Unlike the *kapri,* the *mantiyu* do not live in big, abandoned houses, but underneath tall trees. They sleep standing, not lying down. They are friendly and helpful. Sometimes the *mantiyu* cannot be seen, but they can be heard. Those who have seen the *mantiyu* describes them as big, broad-shouldered, and muscular. They measure more than 10 feet high. The male *mantiyu* do not wear clothing except, occasionally, breechclouts. They have big scrota similar to those of goats and carabaos. They wear their hair long. The female *mantiyu* are likewise scantily dressed.

The *kama²kama²* are small, humanlike creatures with long beards and long nails. They live in small groups near the thickets. The *kama²kama²* are often seen playing with children. They pinch the offender when unduly harmed or angered. In the field, my informants would often show me bruises which they identified as nail marks of the *kamaᵓkamaᵓ*. Similar to the *kamaᵓkamaᵓ* in features, although big in size, are the *sigbin*. They have long white beards and fierce-looking eyes. This group of supernatural beings can be seen only during Holy Week. They go around the barrio "in search for children, whom they butcher for charms. It is said that the heart of small children are good talisman." Malitbog mothers are keen in keeping their children indoors during Holy Week.

The most feared persons with supernatural powers are the *ᵓaswang*. They are capable of changing themselves into any form they desire. They stay in secluded portions of the barrio trail and wait for their victims. I have recorded more than 200 cases narrated by people who claimed to have seen and have been attacked by the *ᵓaswang*. Here is a case.

> Ramon and his friends serenaded Agoy's daughter one bright moonlit night. When he returned home after this romantic episode, he complained of a severe headache. He requested his mother to massage his forehead. A few minutes later, Ramon was delirious with fever, and by morning he was critically ill: his skin turned yellowish; his nails were ash colored; he had a very high fever.
>
> The *baylan* was called and he diagnosed the illness as caused by the workings of the *ᵓaswang*. He requested Ramon's father to secure the following: *kalawag*, ginger, and *bunlaw* [all are known medicinal plants]. The *kalawag* and ginger were sliced and two sets were prepared, each set consisted of seven slices. The *baylan* fumigated the patient with incense and chanted the magic prayers. Then he poulticed the ritual paraphernalia around Ramon's forehead. The *bunlaw* leaves were applied around the stomach.
>
> By noontime, Ramon was able to rest and to go to sleep. In the evening, he became delirious again. So the *baylan* told the patient's father to build a bonfire underneath the house and to keep watch for the *ᵓaswang*. By midnight, as he kept watch over the fire, the old man felt two strong arms around him. He moved to free himself, but it was too late; the *ᵓaswang* had pinioned him tightly. He tried to shout, but he could not say a word—the *ᵓaswang* had cast a charm on him, known as *lupay*. He struggled hard and the noise brought the *baylan* and the men in the house running down. The *ᵓaswang* released the old man and ran away. The *baylan* threw feathers and rubber into the fire. Suddenly they heard a loud and clear sound of *tiktik*. The *ᵓaswang* went away. Ramon recovered from his illness.

CHILDHOOD TRAINING PARALLELS

Malitbog adult preternatural experiences seem to mirror a great deal of the early training practices. In the previous chapters, I have noted that early childhood disciplines take the form of frightening. Physical punishment are resorted to only after the child shows apparent disregard for adult orders. Frightening takes various forms. Most common is frightening the child with preternatural beings, especially the *kamaᵓkamaᵓ*, the *kapri*, and the *ᵓaswang*. Adult members of the family frequently say, "Be silent or the *ᵓaswang* will come to take you." The crying child's attention is often called to imaginary noises, odors, or images in order to make him stop crying. "Did you hear that? Listen—there—there—huh, I am afraid. Now stop crying or the *wakwak* will take you away."

Sometimes an old man or woman is called to frighten the child. Ghosts and *kapri* are also mentioned, and these are associated with the old man or woman. If frightening is not successful, the caretaker hides behind the walls and makes a lot of noise or peeps through the slits and makes faces, all designed to make the child stop crying. Threat of castration is another very common form of frightening the child. The old man who sees the child cry or misbehaves will say, "Huh—stop crying or I will castrate you."

As the child grows up, he is introduced to another form of social control. Evenings are used for telling stories. The basic elements—that is, images, noise, smell, and so forth—of verbal threats are elaborated in the form of tales about environmental spirits, culture heroes, legends, and "actual experiences" of living persons in the barrio. Places where the encounters with preternatural beings have taken place are identified; and each event and each preternatural being is given specific linguistic definition so that the hearer can follow the trend of the story.

I have listened to most of the preternatural experiences which adult Malitbog farmers tell, and I have made children of different age levels identify the supernatural beings for me. It is interesting to note that children between five and eight years old describe these anthropomorphic beings in terms of actual human forms, usually old men and women. These "beings" live in the barrio. They are pictured as aggressive people who like to cut and eat innards of children. They appear both at night and at noontime.

Between ages eight and ten, children identify these preternatural beings as powerful persons who can transform themselves into any form of creatures or animals like pigs, dogs, goats, cats, and so on. They live in a different, though similar, world, to that of the humans. They cannot be killed. Entrance into the supernatural world is through the underground tunnels (known as *bungalog*), behind anthills, springs, and big trees. Distinctions between malevolent and benevolent spirits are mentioned. They not only carry off disobedient children but they also attack adults. Most of the children say that these preternatural beings often appear at night and are preceded by such sounds as *wakwak, tiktik,* and others.

From ten years to adolescence these anthropomorphic personifications become alive and dangerous. They are said to participate actively in human affairs. They are pictured as physically more aggressive, "imbued with mystical powers and bent upon causing death and disease." Many experiences are cited to document the veracity of the existence of these supernatural beings. Everyone is concerned about them, especially when someone is sick or when someone has recently died. Nocturnal visits by these supernatural beings, including tactile experiences with ghosts, are narrated.

In other words, those events that appear in adult experiences and those concepts that occur in adult thinking are also themes of childhood training practices.

13 / Death and burial

MANY CONCEPTS in adult experiences and childhood training are crystallized, as indicated in the previous chapter, in critical life situations occurring in the barrio. One of these life crises is death. Here the tie-up between perceived supernatural realities and actual human affairs emerges. The child learns about death, the causes of death, and how the system of obligations via kin are activated by participating in and observing what the adults do in such situations. In other words, death and burial, as part of the life cycle, round out the traditional education of the child. Thus even before he becomes an adult member of the community, an average Malitbog boy or girl knows what to do when someone dies.

CONCEPT OF DEATH

Death is viewed by the people in Malitbog as the end of mortal existence, but not of life itself, because even after death the relationship between the departed and the living continues. This concept is often transmitted to children through folktales. During evenings I have seen children gather around their grandmother or mother and listen to stories about death or explanations of why so-and-so died. Mal'am Ebi, for example, explained to her grandchildren who gathered around her one evening that "death is a point in time when man departs from the land of the living to the region of the dead." She pointed out that actually "it is not an end; it is a passage from one existence to another. The relationship between the living people and the spirits of the dead continue. That is why it is necessary that we pray and perform the rituals in honor of the spirits of our ancestors. If we do not do so, then they will be angry and will harm the spirit of your father." The children's father died three weeks before I arrived in Malitbog.

Death is caused by a number of factors which can be grouped together into (1) natural causes, such as old age; (2) accidents and murder; and (3) the workings of the supernatural beings. Accidents and murder are clearly understood as caused by injuries of the vital organs of the body. However, the circumstances surrounding them are often viewed in terms of the active participation of the supernatural beings in the affairs of man. A curse, for example, is enough to provoke the supernatural beings to plot circumstances that will lead to the death of an individual. As Teryung explained to a group of youngsters and adults who were gathered in his yard

111

roasting corn: "You know why Kadyo died? First, he nearly killed his father when they quarreled. The old man cursed him. Second, he harmed the *lulid* [a big earth-worm believed to be the pet of the environmental spirits] which he found in his field. Because of these acts he met an untimely death. I am sure of that. All of you know him—he was a healthy, big man. Why did he die suddenly? Because he was cursed by his father." Badong was found dead by his wife beside her when she woke up one morning.

Fate is another determiner of death and no one can give direction or control over his fate; he is wielded by it.

Death due to the workings of supernatural beings takes place only after a person has suffered an illness. Two most common illness are *sininda?* (to be hit by the spirits) and *?inaswang* (to be attacked by a witch). All other diseases are minor variations of these two pervasive ones.

The *sininda?* is cast by the spirits through the *burulakaw,* a powerful malevolent deity. He appears in the form of a bird, with flaming tail which looks like a ball of fire. He can only be seen during midday. The illness due to *sininda?* is charac-terized by profuse sweating, high fever, hallucination, delirium, headache, acute stomachache, and sometimes nausea. Here is one case.

> Lucing and her sister, Caridad, were gathering vegetables in the field. It was high noon and the sun was very hot. The breeze was dry and warm. Suddenly, Lucing called out to her sister that she saw something bright that swiftly passed by. Caridad said she saw nothing.
>
> When the sisters returned home, Lucing complained of severe headache. She was pale, but their mother thought she had an ordinary headache, so no particular attention was given to her. Lucing went to sleep without eating her lunch.
>
> Waking up late in the afternoon, she complained of the same splitting head-ache. Her face was very red. She had, by this time, a very high fever. The mother massaged her body and rubbed pounded ginger on it, but this did not help. By the evening she was delirious, and by midnight she started vomiting blood. The *baylan* was called, but he said Lucing was beyond help; he should have been called earlier. The girl died the following morning.
>
> Persons who were in the field during that unfortunate noontime confirmed Lucing's report that a *burulakaw* was seen in the area. The *baylan* also diagnosed the cause of death as *sininda?*.

Another popular etiology of illness is *?inaswang.* It is due to the charms cast onto the victum by the *?aswang.* The characteristic features of the illness are fever, stomachache, diarrhea, headache, muscle pains, chest pain, and restlessness. Only the *baylan* can cure the *?aswang* ailment (for case study see, earlier in this chapter, the section "Visual Experiences, Tactile phenomenon."

Aside from *sininda?* and *?inaswang,* other causes of death are attributed to the spirits of the trees and springs. These supernatural beings are known as *tumawo.* They inhabit the headwaters of the creek, bowers of trees, cliffs, boulders, and springs. The case of Consoling is often narrated by the people in the barrio to illus-trate the veracity of the *tumawo.* A *tumawo* courted her and, on one occasion, he invited the girl to his place. Because the *tumawo* appeared as a handsome young man, Consoling accepted, and once in the house she ate the food offered. She never came back. Some farmers say Consoling died; others say she is still alive. At any rate, Malitbog mothers often warn their children not to accept food from strangers:

"They might *tumawo* and you will simply disappear. That is what happened to Consoling."

BURIAL PRACTICES

When a person becomes critically ill and about to die, an older woman who is well versed in Christian prayers is called to perform the ritual known as *pahisus.* This consists of helping the sick person cross himself and kiss the crucifix. The people, who are mostly Roman Catholics and Protestants, believe that Christian prayers are more powerful than indigenous prayers in helping an individual die peacefully and in insuring his "entrance to Heaven." Moreover, the prayers can drive away the evil spirits from the house. Children learn these prayers and sometimes participate in the *pahisus* ritual. Another rite is performed immediately after the *pahisus* and this consists of men slashing bolos around the house, aimed at killing the spirits which caused the death of the person. I saw this ritual performed in February 1964 when Badong, a neighbor of my host, died of a lingering illness diagnosed by the local herb-medicine man as caused by the *maligno* (evil spirits).

When the three women who were in constant vigil over Badong noted that he was no longer breathing, they gave a piercing cry: "Badonnnnng huhu Badong is gone huhuhuhuhuh. . . . Oh Badong why did you have to leave us huhuhuhuh. . . ." This wailing lasted for about an hour. The cry was heard all over the barrio, and Badong's relatives stopped working. They all went to the house, and many women joined in the wailing and crying session. Children also cried; there was a noisy commotion in the house.

Order was restored when Mal?am Marsilina and Mal?am Pederiko, Badong's parents, regained composure. They ordered the women to stop crying and to clear the room. Mal?am Marsilina called her oldest daughter and told her to boil water. The children were also ordered to gather fuel and to fetch water from the well. Someone went to get enough *kalawag* (a kind of herbaceous plant with yellow tubers) and vinegar. Mal?am Marsilina went inside a small room and reached for the *lagban* (open end of the wall post) and took a small bottle containing native incense and fine feathers from heron's wings. The women took off Badong's clothes and gave the corpse a sponge bath. Mal?am Pederiko came in with a cupful of juice from the *gaway·gaway* (a kind of tree) bark and he forced it into the dead man's mouth. It is believed that the decoction will prevent rapid internal decay.

Younger women came with blankets and Badong's corpse was covered with it after the sponge bath. A plateful of live embers was brought in and Mal?am Marsilina dropped several pieces of incense into the embers. The plate was first placed underneath the head, then on the breast, or the buttocks, and on the feet. After this, the plate was placed underneath the bed so that the body would be fumigated for some time. A group of young men pounded a quantity of *kalawag,* which was later rubbed all over the body of the dead man. This was done, according to informants, in order to give the corpse a yellowish color and to delay the decay of the flesh.

While the old women were attending to the corpse, the other members of the household secured candles and portraits of saints which were later to hang on the walls of the room. An improvised partition was constructed out of an old blanket. The corpse was placed on a bed and a piece of clean cloth was wound around the chin, the two ends being knotted on top of the crown of the head. The hands were brought to a clasping position over the chest. The head and the chest were next braced a little by a pile of pillows. The candles were lighted and the women and children prayed the novena. A tin plate was placed on top of a chair near the bed. Visitors who came—relatives and friends—put in it their *limus* (contribution) to the dead.

In the meantime everybody was busy in the kitchen. Mal?am Pederiko sent his grandchildren to notify the relatives who were living in the barrio. The big boys were ordered to notify those kin who were living in neighboring towns. A group of men went to the nearby rice mill and ground two sacks of *palay;* another group butchered a pig. Children were sent to borrow pots and frying pans from neighbors. An improvised shed, known as *palayas,* was built in the backyard, and cooking was started. Older boys went to fetch water and to gather fuel. Small children lingered around, both in the kitchen and at the door of the room where the corpse laid in state.

The *laraw* ceremony was performed by the oldest member of the group. Members of the household were enjoined during the ceremony to refrain from making too much noise, from fighting, and from taking a bath for nine days. Novenas were said continuously until midnight. The older men and women did not sleep; they kept vigil over the dead. Early in the following day Mal?am Pederiko sent four men to the *poblacion* to purchase a coffin, which was not delivered until the next day. When the coffin arrived, the corpse was transferred into it. The head portion of the coffin was not covered so that relatives who came late had a chance to take a last look at Badong.

Burial took place on the third day. The corpse was brought down from the house by unmarried men. This was done, according to informants, "to prevent the occurrence of another death in the barrio, especially in the families of those who helped carry the dead from the house to the cemetery." Women cried and wailed as the coffin was covered and lifted out of the door. An old woman poured water over the threshold and another swept the ladder steps with an ?agdaw (a kind of plant) branch, as soon as the coffin reached the ground. The bed on which Badong was placed while lying in state was also carried down the house and put under the heat of the sun.

The coffin was tied to two bamboo poles and was carried by four men. Men, women, and children followed the bier. Upon reaching the *poblacion,* the funeral procession was arranged; small children carrying flowers were asked to walk ahead. They were followed by adults. A piece of black cloth was placed on top of the coffin. All women wore black dress; those who were not able to acquire one right away wore white dresses and black veils. The women also carried candles and prayed as they walked.

The bells were rung as soon as the funeral procession entered the church. For this service, Badong's family paid P 10.00 (about $2.50 U.S. currency). In the church, the coffin was laid before the altar and four stands with lighted candles were placed around it. The cover was removed and the priest performed the last Christian rite.

After this ceremony, the coffin was covered and brought to the cemetery. More wailing and crying characterized the lowering of the coffin into the grave. The people were not allowed to leave until the grave was filled.

A wake, locally known as *bilasyun,* followed the burial. Many attended this occasion in order to comfort and to reassure the bereaved family that their sorrows are shared. The wake took place for nine consecutive nights, during which novenas for the eternal repose of the dead was said. Parlor games were also played. These were participated in both by the adults and children. On the ninth night another ceremony known as *damag* was held. The purpose of the *damag* was twofold: to pray for the eternal repose of the soul of the dead man, and to break the mourning taboo which the bereaved family observed in deference to the dead. After this ninth day the members of the family can resume normal activities—they can take baths and do hard work.

14 / Summing up: tradition and the learning process

IN THE INTRODUCTION I stated that this book is intended as a case study in education. To discover how learning and transmission of culture take place, I have focused much attention on the life cycle. Ruth Benedict (1938) put this approach in context when she argued that all cultures must deal in one way or another with the cycle of growth from infancy to adulthood:

> Every man who rounds out his human potentialities, must have been a son first and a father later and the two roles are physiologically in great contrast; he must first have been dependent upon others for his very existence and later he must provide much security for others (1938:161).

How the individual is prepared for these various roles depends upon the training he receives from other people as he grows up. In some societies much of the training is done in formally established institutions like the school, the college, or the university; in others the skills are learned through participation in community affairs. In Malitbog only a fraction of the child's training is acquired in school; most of his skills are learned at home through instruction received informally from his elders, siblings, playmates, and work companions. This kind of training starts very early. Even before the child can fully respond to verbalization, his parents or any adult members of the family talk to him as though he were already grown up. When he cries, the mother quiets him down by scolding someone else for having caused his discomfort.

As the child grows older, he starts to label objects around him and to discriminate one from the other. The manner in which he achieves this is determined by the way the objects are, in turn, differentiated for him by his parents, brothers, sisters, or any adult member of the family. In a word, the child's capacity to organize his choice patterns follows the general educational principles of watching, listening, and doing, all of which are dependent upon the mode of reciprocal responses obtaining between him and other people through verbal and symbolic communications.

There is indeed no other factor which so much conditions the social behavior of the child or the role he must play in the social system as the expectation of adults. In Malitbog, adult expectations rest on two general cultural assumptions. One of these is the belief that children are gifts from God, grace from Heaven. Hence they are much desired and enjoyed, and the idea of birth control is frowned upon. Children are likewise regarded in practical terms as "some kind of investment for the future. The more children a person has, the more there will be upon whom he can depend for support in old age." Thus children, even at an early age, are expected to contribute to the family larder. Boys help their father in his economic activities and they are regarded by him as "my right-hand men." The girls assist the mother in her household chores.

The other basic assumption in Malitbog culture is the concept that children are born with specific traits and no amount of education or training can restructure these characteristics. If the child is good—that is, quiet, industrious, obedient, and so forth—this is not due to the training he receives at home or in school, but to the fact that he is born with these traits already set in him. If he turns out to be bad— that is, a troublemaker, disobedient, undependable, and the like—he must have inherited the bad qualities from either of his parents or ancestors.

It must not be construed, however, that because of these cultural assumptions punishment (verbal or physical) is absent in Malitbog. Punishment takes the form of scolding, a sharp tone of voice, withholding affection, beating, threatening, and frightening. Rewards such as verbal praise, smiles, approving nods, and so forth, complement punishment as a form of social control. Such stern admonitions as "don't do this," "don't do that," and "don't be naughty" daily impress on the child the idea that certain actions are carried out according to some recognized procedure.

As he begins to participate in the adult world, the child learns further that he can engage in harmonious relations with other members of the community through the reckoning of kinship ties which exist between them. By the use of specific terms he can anticipate the role(s) each member of the group will play on almost all occasions and how he himself should act correspondingly. By this device, too, he can distinguish one kinsman from another. Father is thus terminologically distinguished from mother's brother, and mother is likewise distinguished from father's sister, even if he addresses all of them directly in similar kinship terms. Grandparents are also terminologically set apart. Cousins are grouped and differentiated as first, second, third, fourth cousins, and so on. Seen from this perspective, kinship terms are used to specify positions, establish an individual's social identity, and prescribe appropriate modes of behavior. Thus a child can joke with persons whom he calls grandfather or grandmother, but not those whom he addresses as father or mother. His obligations and privileges are also regulated by the kind of relationship he has with his kin. That is, he can expect more assistance from his first cousins in time of need than he could from his fourth or fifth cousins. In turn, he is obligated to help them more than he is expected to attend to the problems of his distant kin.

The classification of kinsmen inherent in the kinship terms used, the definition of statuses as specified by the chosen term, and the appropriate behavior evoked by each term as applied to specific persons all tend to regulate the social life of the people of Malitbog and prescribe for them the manner in which they should behave toward every other kinsman. It is natural that experience should be organized and interpreted in terms of kinship in a small community of kinsmen with whom interaction is rather rigidly defined by kinship. David Schneider and George Homans (1957:1194–1208) are of the opinion that the

> kinship system as a whole is therefore a socialization device, a "child-training practice," if you will, which looms considerably larger than any given child-train-

ing practice like weaning or toilet training or aggression control. . . . Where it may be difficult to place an exact socialization value on weaning as such, it is much less difficult to discover the socialization values of a whole kinship system.

Reinforcing this network of relationships is a complex set of norms and values which the people observe in carrying out their daily interactions. These norms and values function as built-in mechanisms which make the system work. The child learns this early in life. Among these behavioral norms are reciprocal exchange of food and services, emphasis on word of honor (*amor propio*) and self-esteem, and a set of supernaturally oriented forms of social control. These established standards constitute the fundamental educational mechanisms that mold an individual into an acceptable member of Malitbog society. Consciously or unconsciously the child finds himself in recurrent situations where he is rewarded when he observes these norms and values and is punished when he disobeys them, and as he internalizes these codes of conduct, they, in turn, become guidelines on which he bases his judgments when met with problems which call for on-the-spot decisions in later life.

The patterning of these normative behaviors is further legitimized by the belief in the sanctioning powers of the supernatural beings which maintain active interests in the affairs of men. These nonhumans cause illness and misfortunes to those who do not observe the rules of conduct; they reward those who are obedient and faithful. Thus the people must square accounts with the spirits by observing the conventional ways of behavior if they are to live in security and peace in the barrio. The people view their society as a small part of a wider natural-social universe inhabited partly by spirits and partly by human beings. The social prescriptions for so many human actions are felt to come from metaphysical demands. The pattern of life is fixed because it is part of the general order of the universe, and even if this is hardly understood and regarded as mysterious, it is nevertheless accepted as invariant and regular.

Of course it can be argued in this connection that many childhood experiences are easily unlearned and forgotten in the process of growing up, warranting an evaluation of emphasis as to their significance in understanding adult behavior. This is true, and I do not deny the influence of the intervening variables which tend to blur or cover up the primal scenes of early experiences. However, it is equally true, especially in a more or less culturally homogeneous society like Malitbog that unlearning and forgetting childhood experiences are not easily achieved. In fact, what happens is that these experiences—including acquired norms, ideas, and predispositions—are reinforced and validated by continuous hearing of accounts told and retold as actual events by adult members.

These traditional Malitbog ways constitute the background against which the children grow up. Thus, in spite of the fact that many children have gone to school, it does not take long before a majority of them forget whatever skills they learn there. This is because there is apparently no continuity between classroom instruction and the requirements of community life outside of it. The educational experiences of children outside of the classroom have practical value in terms of action processes obtaining in day-to-day life and they fit into the general pattern of local expectations about the role of a child at home. In contrast, instruction in school is outlined in specific ways, imparted to the child in serried ranks within the classroom, and this instruction does not have immediate, practical usefulness in terms of actual needs. Thus, what is learned in school is easily forgotten. If modern education has to be a vehicle for social and cultural change, educators must reckon with the significance of *continuity* between classroom instruction and community life where the school operates. Malitbog is a case that demonstrates why this is necessary.

Glossary

AFFINES: relatives by marriage.

BILATERAL KINSHIP: reckoning or tracing kin relationship equally from both the father's and the mother's sides.

CONSANGUINEAL: relatives by blood.

CROSS COUSINS: children of siblings of different sex.

CURRICULUM: a course of study; all the courses of study in an educational institution.

DYADIC RELATIONS: interactions of two persons in a more or less patterned manner.

ENCULTURATION: the process of learning a tradition.

FAMILY OF ORIENTATION: one in which a person is born and reared.

FAMILY OF PROCREATION: one that an individual forms by marriage.

PERSONAL KINDRED: close relatives surrounding a person.

PARALLEL COUSINS: children of siblings of the same sex.

REFERENTIAL TERMS: terms used refer to a relative when talking to someone else about him.

SIBLINGS: brothers and sisters.

SOCIALIZATION: the process of becoming a member of the society.

VOCATIVE: terms used when speaking directly to a relative.

References and recommended reading

BENEDICT, RUTH, "Continuities and Discontinuities in Cultural Conditioning," *Psychiatry,* Vol. I (May 1938), pp. 160–167.
A discussion about a certain relationship between culture and child training.

EGGAN, DOROTHY, "Instruction and Affect in Hopi Cultural Continuity," *Southwestern Journal of Anthropology.* Vol. XII (Winter 1956), pp. 347–370.
Examines the educational process in Hopi society.

FOX, ROBERT, "Social Organization," in *Area Handbook on the Philippines,* Vol. I (4 vols.), edited by Fred Eggan, and others. Chicago: The University of Chicago for the Human Relations Area Files, 1956, pp. 413–470.
A good summary of existing materials on Filipino social organization.

FREEMAN, JOHN, "The Concept of Kindred" *Journal of the Royal Anthropological Institute.* Vol. 91, Part 2 (July to December 1961), pp. 192–220.
An analysis of the concept of kindred.

JOCANO, F. LANDA, *The Traditional World of Malitbog: A Study of Community Development and Culture Change in a Philippine Barrio.* Quezon City: Community Development Research Council, 1968.
Describes the problem of introducing a program of directed change in a Philippine barrio.

MEAD, MARGARET, *Growing Up In New Guinea.* New York: New American Library, Inc., 1960.
An excellent study of the process of growing up among the sea-dwelling Manus of the Admiralty Islands, north of New Guinea.

MURDOCK, GEORGE P., *Social Structure.* New York: St. Martin's Press, Inc., 1949.
A basic text on the theory of social structure.

RADCLIFFE-BROWN, A. R. "The Study of Kinship System" in *Structure and Function in Primitive Society.* New York: The Free Press, 1952.
A classic treatment of kinship system.

SCHNEIDER, DAVID, AND GEORGE A. HOMANS, "Kinship Terminology and the American Kinship System," *American Anthropologist.* Vol. 57, No. 6 (December 1955), pp. 1194–1208.
An excellent analysis of American kinship system as a socialization device.

SHIBUTANI, TAMOTSU, *Society and Personality: An Interactionist Approach to Social Psychology.* Englewood Cliffs, N.J.: Prentice-Hall, Inc., 1961.
A general text on social psychology.

SPINDLER, GEORGE, ed. *Culture and Education: Anthropological Approaches.* New York: Holt, Rinehart, and Winston, Inc., 1963.
Considers ways in which anthropology can contribute to the understanding of educational process.

WHITING, BEATRICE, ed. *Six Cultures: Studies on Child Rearing.* New York: John Wiley & Sons, Inc., 1963.
A descriptive monograph on child training in six different cultures written by scholars from different disciplines. Includes a section on the Philippines.

Date Due